SAY MORE

Lessons from Work,
the White House, and the World

JEN PSAKI

SCRIBNER
New York   London   Toronto   Sydney   New Delhi

Scribner
An Imprint of Simon & Schuster, LLC
1230 Avenue of the Americas
New York, NY 10020

First Scribner hardcover edition May 2024

SCRIBNER and design are trademarks of Simon & Schuster, LLC

Simon & Schuster: Celebrating 100 Years of Publishing in 2024

For information about special discounts for bulk purchases, please contact Simon & Schuster Special Sales at 1-866-506-1949 or business@simonandschuster.com.

The Simon & Schuster Speakers Bureau can bring authors to your live event. For more information, or to book an event, contact the Simon & Schuster Speakers Bureau at 1-866-248-3049 or visit our website at www.simonspeakers.com.

Interior design by Jaime Putorti

Manufactured in the United States of America

10 9 8 7 6 5 4 3 2 1

Library of Congress Cataloging-in-Publication Data has been applied for.

ISBN 978-1-6680-1985-6
ISBN 978-1-6680-1987-0 (ebook)

TO VIVI AND MATTHEW

As you go out into the world,
I hope you are always kind,
and curious, and also know how to say more.

Contents

My First Press Briefing   *1*

1. Remember When That Nice Man Won the Election?   *11*

   On identifying and connecting with your audience through
   emotion, humor, and common ground

2. What If I Don't Know Enough about Venezuela?   *29*

   On the importance of research, planning, practice, and
   scripting, to decrease anxiety and avoid insulting famous rappers

3. That's Not Credible!   *49*

   On giving and receiving feedback gracefully, tactfully,
   and without disrupting international peace agreements

**4. If You Can't Say Anything Nice,
   You Still Have to Say Something**   *73*

   On having tough conversations with your family,
   your colleagues, and Joe Biden

5. What the Heck Is a "Non-Filer"?   *95*

   On the importance of building and conveying trust,
   credibility, and expertise as a communicator

6. When to Serve a PsakiBomb   *115*

   On communicating across divides,
   at home and with Fox News

7. A Punch Line China Would Find Funny   *131*

   On making mistakes, issuing clarifications,
   correcting yourself, and apologizing

8. Kindergarten Open House on the Worst Day
   in the White House   *147*

   On saying no, explaining your boundaries,
   and knowing how to quit

9. Say Less   *163*

   On managing what you're not supposed to say and keeping
   classified information to yourself

10. Russia Says You're Getting Fired?   *179*

   On dealing with rumors, gossip, and bullying,
   from Vladimir Putin or your office frenemy

11. Say More   *199*

   How to listen actively and attentively, whether networking,
   at dinner, or conducting an interview on television

Taking Questions   *215*

   On answering tough questions effectively and honestly

Acknowledgments   *219*

Notes   *223*

Photo Credits   *225*

SAY MORE

My First Press Briefing

As calm as I may have looked at my first White House briefing, several cups of coffee and lots of practice preceded this photo.

It was one of the most important days of my career, and I was on my way to the zoo. On January 20, 2021, Joe Biden was being sworn in as the forty-sixth president of the United States, and I was about to start my job as White House press secretary. As a security precaution following the January 6 attack on the Capitol, a perimeter had been set up around the White House complex, which meant the team starting work that day had to meet off-site and take buses to our new office. We boarded buses at the National Zoo. I arrived shortly before 11:00 a.m. and checked in. And, yes, the zoo was open, but since it was the middle of January we weren't caught up in the typical warm-weather rush of families trying to get a glimpse of the pandas.

While our buses navigated the detours set up in place for the event, we all pulled up the inauguration on our phones to watch Joe Biden take the oath of office. The White House press secretary would typically attend the inauguration, but there had never been a press briefing on Inauguration Day before and I needed to prepare. After everything the country had been through over the previous four years, it was surreal to be watching such a momentous event on such a tiny screen. Cell service wasn't great. I squinted. Lady Gaga was singing the national anthem—what was on her dress? An eagle? A golden . . . plane? On my small phone screen, it kind of looked like a plane. No—a dove.

But I couldn't be distracted by zoo animals or any animals—I had work to do. I would be giving my first briefing as press secretary that night during prime time. We were realizing that part of the reason there had never been a briefing on Inauguration Day before was due to logistics. One funny detail about working at the White House is that, until noon on Inauguration Day, the previous president and their team occupy the building. So, with the possible exception of some national security staff, I and the rest of Biden's senior officials were locked out until 12:00 p.m. I would be going live just seven hours later. The COVID-19 pandemic was still raging, so we were all wearing masks. While we had been doing regular practice briefings for a few weeks, most had been over Zoom due to the security precautions downtown. Stepping up to the podium on live television was going to be different from answering questions over a computer screen balanced on a pile of books, from my house, in my slippers.

In early January, we had decided it was vital to speak to the press on Inauguration Day. Beginning with Trump's former press secretary Sean Spicer's infamous first briefing a few days after the inauguration (more on this later) in which he bragged, despite all statistical and photographic evidence, that Trump's swearing-in had seen "the largest audience to ever witness an inauguration, period," the Trump administration had cultivated a relationship of animosity and distrust with the press. We wanted to reset the tone in the briefing room and hopefully take some of the venom out of our exchanges. I had always valued the role of reporters and the media, even on days when things were tense, and I wanted to convey this message to the White House press corps. We were there to provide them with information, to the best of our ability, so that they could report on the work of the president and the White House to the public.

After the senior staff and I disembarked from our zoo buses and trudged, with security, through the deserted streets of downtown DC, the afternoon was a whirlwind: I spent too long trying and failing to log into my new work computer and opening cabinets and closets in disbelief that I was moving into the press secretary office. Then I had a meeting in the Oval Office with a group of the president's senior advisors to discuss how I would characterize the events of that day in my evening briefing.

One of my most important early tasks was to establish my credibility by conveying that I had a connection with the president and would be engaging with him on a daily basis. I was new to the Biden team, and while I had worked with White House reporters during my time in the Obama administration, I needed to prove I was able to reliably and effectively speak on behalf of the president. I'd spent the weeks before preparing for all manner of questions on policy and politics, but there were a couple of topics I knew the press corps would bring up that were more personal. Stepping into the Oval Office on Inauguration Day brought me immediately back to the final weeks of the Obama administration, when I was serving as the communications director. The furniture and décor were different, but there was something about looking through the back windows of the Oval Office onto the North Lawn that still felt pretty magical.

I asked President Biden if he had read the letter that was tra-
ditional for the departing president to leave behind—it was usually
somewhere easy to find in the Oval Office. Given President Trump's
approach to both the job and his sentiments about this election, we
weren't totally sure he had followed this protocol. "Do you know
where it is?" the president asked. It wasn't on top of the desk. He
began opening drawers.

Finally, he pulled out an envelope. Across the desk, I could see it
was written in scripted penmanship, and it was several pages long. I
waited patiently for President Biden to read it, which took a few minutes. (It really was long.) When he looked up from the letter he deemed
it generous and gracious. Part of my task would be to describe President
Biden's thoughts on this private letter in terms that were respectful but
didn't suggest a warm relationship. We agreed that I would leave the
description as "gracious" when I briefed the press later that evening.
Describing as "generous" any action, even the writing of a letter, by the
former president who had clearly sparked an insurrection felt far too
generous to all of us.

The rest of the afternoon was a blur; I only had brief moments to
feel anxious about what I'd have to do that evening. I was as prepared
as I could be; I knew my message, my audience, and—importantly—
what I was going to wear (an old blue J.Crew dress I had pulled from
my closet). The briefing was being aired live by many networks, so we
wanted to be on time—we didn't want to keep the press corps or the
American people waiting. Before we walked into the briefing room, my
deputy Karine Jean-Pierre and I took a quick moment to shake out the
nerves with a little shoulder shimmy before we opened the blue sliding
doors. Then we walked out onto the podium; according to the official
White House record, I began the briefing at 7:06 p.m.—pretty good
for having just entered the building at lunchtime.

The White House press corps typically asks incoming press secretaries a couple of standard questions during their first briefings. One is about how they view the role and their relationship to the media—did I feel it was my job to serve the president, or the press? The stakes were pretty high. I needed to get the tone right. "There will be moments when we disagree, and there will certainly be days where we even disagree for extensive parts of the briefing," I began.

> *But we have a common goal, which is sharing accurate information with the American people. If the president were standing here with me today, he would say he works for the American people. I work for him, so I also work for the American people. But his objective and his commitment are to bring transparency and truth back to government—to share the truth, even when it's hard to hear. And that's something that I hope to deliver on in this role as well.*

The briefing lasted thirty-one minutes—not that I was counting. When it was over I felt a rush of adrenaline (perhaps the several cups of coffee I had that day contributed and also led to a sleepless night before my second briefing) and then relief. After a meeting with my team to discuss the next day's briefing, I went home. An hour or two later my cell phone flashed a call from an unknown number. I picked up, a little nervous, even though I was pretty sure I hadn't done anything to compromise the American government.

"Jilly's sisters loved it!" I heard President Biden say on the other end of the line. "They thought you were terrific!" This was so touching— a reaction relayed from the extended Biden universe felt more authentic, more real, than a simple compliment from my boss. The First Lady's sisters were my actual audience—I needed to serve, and impress, President Biden and Dr. Jill Biden, but I was also communicating with the press and the wider public at the same time. Before he got off the phone to tend to his many other duties, he added that he felt like I knew his voice. The *New York Times* headline about the briefing signaled I'd done what I set out to do: "Jen Psaki's Debut: No Attacks, No Lectures, No Crowd Size Fixation."

Most jobs don't require such a dramatic public debut. But the communication skills I used to prepare for and execute this first briefing are applicable to a wide range of life experiences, whether you're a parent talking to a teacher about your preschooler, a friend trying to encourage a coworker to take a risk, or a young female staffer trying to convince the most powerful man in the world what he might want to include in his State of the Union address.

I know because I've been in each of those rooms, from the parent-teacher conference, to the late-night kitchen table bonding session, to the Oval Office, at moments when the success or failure of a conversation hinged on how we communicated. Sometimes I was pitching an idea; other times I was tasked with listening and responding respectfully. And although I think I'm good at communicating now, I wasn't always. Becoming a strong communicator means being open to screwing up, and improving after making mistakes; it requires listening to feedback both good and bad; and it requires a lot of practice.

My career in politics started when I was twenty-three and decided to move to Des Moines because I thought I might enjoy working for the Iowa Democratic Party. I spent the next six months getting a crash course in communication, knocking on doors and asking people whom they planned to vote for and why. In the more than two decades since, I've worked on countless political races, including three presidential campaigns, served as a spokesperson for the secretary of state and two presidents, and now anchor a Sunday morning and Monday prime-time hour-long news show on MSNBC. Over those years I have learned, sometimes the hard way, that knowing your audience is almost as important as knowing your material (which is, just to be super clear, also important); that difficult conversations are best approached head-on; that speaking across different beliefs requires grace, tact, and a willingness to give up the fantasy of "winning" in favor of the realistic goal of understanding; that the ability to both give and receive feedback is rarer than you think; and that really listening doesn't mean just sitting back and waiting for what you want to hear.

What I know about communication I've picked up from observing others and from a lot of practice. I've collected advice from experts working high-stress, high-profile jobs, but I've also learned a lot from people who have never worked in government or media: my mother, my husband, my sisters and their partners, our friends, and even my own children have taught me invaluable lessons about how best to express myself, and about how to make others comfortable expressing themselves, too. I've had to communicate to the American public when there were huge, global stakes, and I've had to try to explain to a toddler why he should give up his pacifier when he *really* doesn't want to.

The lessons from each encounter turn out to be surprisingly similar. That's why in the pages to come I've included stories from my days working for Barack Obama, Joe Biden, and John Kerry, as well as from my personal life. Many of them are not flattering—like the time I accidentally cc'd the entire Iowa press corps on an email about a political opponent. But they all reveal something important about becoming a successful communicator.

I'll warn you: much of the advice in this book runs counter to the ways we tend to interact in the present moment. After two decades of social media, a few years of a pandemic, and an ex-president seemingly determined to start, rather than end, conflicts, our communication skills have deteriorated—we find it hard to believe we might have something in common with people outside our inner circle, we get nervous when a conversation requires a live, spontaneous response, and we're also very, very distracted. We have a hard time being present. More than ever, people of all ages prefer to text instead of talk. We monologue more and dialogue less. While I don't believe all technology is toxic—where would we be if we couldn't FaceTime with friends and grandparents living across the country?—I do believe the most powerful conversations happen in person.

Of course, my experiences will be different from yours. I've had to routinely communicate with rooms full of (at times hostile) reporters, the president, a multitude of high-ranking officials, and a range of brilliant colleagues, but also my family—my kids, asking why I couldn't pick them up from school, or my husband, when I told him for the umpteenth time that I would be gone for the next few days because I had yet another business trip (turns out the words "Air Force One" get old pretty quickly when you're the one stuck at home changing diapers). Sometimes I had to talk to these people at the same time. Working in politics and government also requires dealing with more volatile topics, and personalities, than this rather rosy portrait of my first appearance on the podium as press secretary suggests. I have had many rough moments of public speaking, including when I inadvertently made a joke about an important national security agency, and when Russian media targeted me with an onslaught of abuse and misinformation.

How we define successful communication varies by the objective, participants, and subject. If I ask my sister to bring a dessert when she comes over for a barbeque, the goal is pretty self-explanatory, and the metric for success is simple. We all navigate these straightforward exchanges on a daily basis. But if I ask my husband to sit down and discuss the next year of our work and personal commitments, we aren't necessarily going to end up with everything resolved and annotated neatly on a piece of paper or set in stone on the calendar. He might say, "It's important to me that we have a date night every month, and I want to take an annual trip with my guy friends." I might say, "It's important to me that we have my family over for pizza night at least twice a month, and also I want to plan some time with just the two of us and the kids." The goal of that conversation is not to necessarily schedule every single event and vacation for the next twelve months, but to air things out, to discuss the whys, so that across subsequent conversations we can nail down the hows and whens. That is successful communication: an ongoing process, with a lot of moving parts.

Yet there are some constants no matter whom you're talking to. In my first White House press briefing, I emphasized that I was not an enemy: the reporters and I had a common goal. In every conversation, you and the people you are engaging with also have a common goal: to leave the encounter feeling better than you started, to make yourself heard and to hear others in return. This book is not just about how to communicate publicly, though I do write a lot about that. It is about how to say more—in your conversations with your family, your friends, your colleagues, and people with whom you disagree. That doesn't mean talking louder or using more words; it means communicating with greater impact.

So put down your phone (unless you are reading this book on your phone and then that's fine) and start reading.

1

Remember When That Nice Man Won the Election?

On identifying and connecting with your audience through emotion, humor, and common ground

When I took the job as press secretary, I told my daughter this nice man had asked me to work with him. Here is President Biden calling my dad (whose grandfather immigrated from Greece) on Greek Independence Day.

The year was 2002, and I somehow found myself working in the admissions office at a for-profit art school. I'd graduated from college two years earlier, and had no idea what I wanted to do with my life so took the first job I was offered. I had worked in politics a little bit during college. In 1999, the summer between my junior and senior years, I interned for Nancy Jacobson, then the national finance director

for Senator Evan Bayh from Indiana. Our office was on Massachusetts Avenue near Union Station in DC, and while I didn't know a ton
about political fundraising (still don't), I knew right away that I loved
the energy of Washington. So a few years later, after spending far too
much soul-sucking time in the art school job that had nothing to do
with public service, I began volunteering for the Arlington Democratic
Party. I mostly stuffed envelopes, but I was apparently very enthusiastic
about it, because one day an older staffer (who was probably about
thirty at the time) came to talk to me. "You seem to like this," he said.
"Maybe you should go work on a campaign."

It didn't take much to convince me that I was ready for a change.
I quit my job, broke up with my boyfriend, and signed up for a training program that would eventually match me with a campaign. I didn't
know a lot about politics, but I knew enough to know that presidential
campaigns always started in Iowa and that was where I wanted to go.
Fortunately, the program placed me in a job with the Iowa Democratic
Party.

Once I'd moved halfway across the country, I was tasked with a job
anyone who has ever worked or volunteered in politics knows well: door
knocking. And some phone banking. I would be going from house to
house, or down a list of names, and talking to potential voters about
the issues they cared about, and what might convince them to cast their
vote for a Democrat in the upcoming election.

At first, I thought this would entail the glamorous skills you see
politicians exhibit on television and in movies: persuasion, charm, ability to cite specific facts. Not quite—though those things would come
in handy. As door knockers, we were given lists of residents, organized
by street, and all the publicly available information about their voting
records. Based on the information we had about each voter, we knew
that some of the people whose afternoons we were interrupting were
probably on the fence about voting for a Democrat, or voting at all. In

most cases, the goal was simply to get them to answer the door, not slam it in our faces, and maybe chat for a few minutes—long enough for us to survey them about their priorities and preferences, and, if we were really, *really* convincing, to encourage them to sign up to receive their ballot by mail. This would ensure that we could then follow up with them in the weeks leading up to the election to confirm that they had voted. We conducted our surveys on a Palm Pilot—the height of modern technology at the time. (For younger readers, a Palm Pilot was like a nineteenth-century version of an iPad, without any of the features.)

We had a lot of information about the registered voters we were trying to reach in each household. But that didn't mean we knew what their views were on any particular issue or even on the candidates, and it was entirely possible that someone who wasn't on our list of voters would answer the door. This meant we had to be flexible and adapt our message on the fly, based on what we could assess in just a few seconds. We had to use clues like body language to figure out how to engage them. This was my first lesson in the importance of knowing your audience, and it played a role in shaping my career.

We surveyed our assigned areas in four-hour blocks, and although I was nervous at first, I'd quickly get psyched up for the prospect of a willing interlocutor after a string of "No one's home" and "Not interested." (Perhaps an early sign of my love of being underestimated. We will talk more about that later.) I was intrigued by the possibility that I might be able to make just one convincing point. And yes, there were weird moments, like the time a man answered the door in his underwear, holding a shotgun. But every house was different, every potential voter a new challenge. My initial objective was always to establish myself as friendly and non-threatening within the first five seconds of an interaction. After that I had to adapt my communication strategy quickly. I talked to people who homeschooled their children, to seniors who offered me iced tea and invited me into their living rooms (you aren't supposed to accept, but I usually did), to people who had lost their jobs. I got a little competitive. Could I gather more information than my fellow door knockers?

Another part of my job was to do what is called candidate tracking, which means showing up at the events of Republicans running for office and videotaping them. My boss was a guy named Mark Daley. He was the communications director for the Iowa Democratic Party and I'd seen him quoted in the *Des Moines Register*. I had a bit of a crush on him. I don't think I knew anything about political communications at the time, but I'd majored in English in college and I loved to read and write. If you asked me then, I probably would have said I thought working on the press team seemed "cool." I was becoming fascinated with the world of media—I was especially interested in the role journalists played in shaping public opinion. Drawing very literally on my experience talking to voters in their homes, I went to my crush's office and knocked on his door.

"I'm a pretty good writer," I said. "If I can ever be helpful to the team, I'd love to learn more about how communications on a campaign works." I cringe when I tell this story now: my level of confidence far exceeded my skill set at the time.

I still don't know exactly why, but he agreed to let me shadow him for a few days. In retrospect, I contributed very little—though I did help organize a protest against Dick Cheney, with a "Halli-bacon" (as in "Halliburton") pig attending as a mascot. Otherwise, I had no idea how to write a press release or talk to a reporter. But I learned a lot, including that I wanted my next campaign job to be on the press team.

After the campaign ended, I went back to the East Coast for a couple of months, but I had my eye on the 2004 presidential campaign (part career ambition, part I had started dating a guy who lived in Iowa). When the time came, I was excited to end up on John Kerry's

team back in Des Moines. My official title was assistant to the state
director, but my coworker and roommate John Liipfert and I liked to
call ourselves the Coheads of Staple Procurement because basically our
jobs were to make sure everyone had what they needed, including office
supplies. Meanwhile, nobody had been hired to do press yet.

Once again, I knocked on a door. "I'm really interested in press," I
told John Norris, who was the state director for John Kerry's Iowa campaign. "Until you hire a communications director, I'd love to help out
in any way I can. I'd love to learn more about it." He gave me a shot.

It would be nice if simply knocking on a door and presenting your
message clearly was all you needed to do to communicate effectively—
whether you're asking your boss for a raise, telling your partner you're
ready to take the next step and move in together, or describing a new
healthcare policy proposal to the White House press corps. In reality, communication is usually much more complicated. Although my
experience knocking on doors and taking voter surveys as a twenty-
three-year-old was very different from speaking on behalf of the State
Department or the president, as I'd have to do much later, those initial
glimpses into how politics work on the ground in Iowa turned out to
be essential for a career in communications. One of the first lessons I
learned campaigning in 2002 was, in many ways, the foundation of all
successful communication: the importance of knowing your audience.
This is the whole idea behind door knocking—it's still considered one
of the best ways to connect with voters even, or especially, now, in an
age of digital media and targeted ads. You have to know your audience
before you have any hope of connecting with them.

Over the last twenty-two years, and several communications jobs,
I've found there are three broad principles of audience engagement to
keep in mind, no matter what your role or whom you're talking to:

determine your target audience, craft your message, and lower any barriers to engagement.

First: identify who your audience is. Most of the time, and
particularly in one-on-one situations, identifying your audience is
straightforward enough—any complication comes from the personalities, and clashing priorities, that may be involved. (Maybe the boss
you're approaching for a raise is only in a good mood about once a
month and you never know when that's going to be; maybe the partner you want to move in with is secretly a neat freak and terrified of
sharing a closet with you.) There are times, though, when identifying
your audience can be harder than it seems. Great communication
skills are most important when there *isn't* a clear yes or no answer—
when solutions, or compromises, might have to expand to fit many
different groups and priorities.

Negotiating among all the different audiences I had to communicate with was a constant during my time as White House press secretary. Whenever I stepped up to the podium to brief the press during the
height of legislative negotiations, I had to pick my priority audience:
Was I addressing the reporters in the room, the members of Congress,
the general public, or my boss, the president of the United States?

The answer is all of the above, but in different ways. I was trying to use the forum of the White House briefing to push President
Biden's agenda forward, so representing his point of view was essen-
tially job #1—if I screwed that up, he had every right to fire me. But
I wasn't speaking *to* President Biden at that moment, just *on behalf
of* him.

As press secretary, I was speaking to the audiences that had a direct
influence on whether the president's agenda was implemented: both
sides of the aisle in Congress, reporters who would shape the public's
views on the bill, and, of course, the public itself. On the flip side of
speaking for but not to my boss, there were the reporters who were

hanging on my every word, oftentimes trying to get me to slip up or say more than I wanted to.

I knew this would be a challenge. Before starting the job, I reached out to several of my predecessors to get their advice—which is also good advice—and many of them, both Democrats and Republicans, offered a version of this point: It's easy to get into a verbal jousting match with reporters in the room, so remember who the target audience is. It may be members of Congress. It may be members of your political party, or the opposing party. It may be people at home interested in information about a natural disaster or a public health crisis. While I always had to keep the press corps in mind because they were the intermediary between me and the public, the reporters in the room were rarely, if ever, my most important audience.

I also couldn't be constantly running after the ball as the press kicked it down the field. As press secretary, or any kind of spokesperson, you'll lose track of larger strategic objectives if you're constantly chasing the day-to-day focus of the people around you. If everyone in the press office were focused on managing stories about Commander Biden, the president's famously naughty German shepherd, for example, because news about the dog's inappropriate behavior always tends to grab media attention, they would fail to drive home the importance of basically any other issue. Everyone loves to hear about the relatively low-stakes drama of Commander's biting criticism of the Secret Service—and that's exactly why the press team can't let themselves get distracted by making that kind of story bigger than it already is.

So: If I wasn't really speaking to the president, or the press, whom was I speaking to, and why? Kelly McGonigal, author of *The Neuroscience of Change*, says that she tries to foreground the best possible outcome for the audience she cares most about. "I'm always thinking, well, whom am I really trying to speak to or reach, and what's the best possible outcome for them?" she writes. "Do I want them to feel a certain way? Do I want them to change their behavior in a certain way? And then I work backwards and I think, what do they need to hear? What do they need to do? What story could I tell that would make that outcome more likely?"

Determining what audience will be your primary focus goes beyond thinking about who might be most affected in a situation, or who might be the most powerful party in the equation. You have to determine which audience—be it one person or 1 million viewers—might provide the sort of engagement that can ultimately, over time, help move your objective forward. You can be the most articulate speaker around, but if you can't figure out who is open to listening to you, and what you need to say in order for them to do so, you might as well not say anything at all.

When the Biden administration was trying to pass the infrastructure bill in 2021, we were walking a tightrope, trying to make the case to both Republicans and Democrats and to address a range of different views within each of those parties. This was a challenge because, with a price tag of $1.2 trillion, it was not a small bill. We decided the best strategy was to talk about benefits the majority of the American people would support: things like funding for improvements to roads, bridges, and airports and expanding high-speed internet access throughout the country. Many of the provisions of the bill were sorely needed, and the legislation had the potential to be truly bipartisan in a way that few big bills had been in recent years. But passing it would be a major win for the Biden administration.

I had a lot of charts and graphs available, which might have been convincing to some groups, but from the podium I couldn't focus on them—when answering questions about the bill I avoided spending too much time on the fine print details that were still being negotiated so that it wouldn't seem like I was attempting to publicly pressure, or shame, any individual congressperson for their lack of support.

(Though a good number of Democrats would have enjoyed me doing just that.) I had to create space so that someone who might take heat for voting in favor of the bill would not be viewed as a traitor among their supporters. I knew that most members of Congress, regardless of their party affiliation, would want to be seen by the people they represented as having acted independently, for the public good—not in cahoots with a president some of those constituents, and nearly every congressional Republican, considered the enemy.

We didn't need (or expect) the vote to be unanimous, so while it was true that in theory my primary audience was everyone in Congress, we had close to zero hope that those on the fringes—especially on the margins of the minority party—were going to be open to engagement. They, too, had their primary audience, and it didn't reward bipartisanship. But we still wanted them to feel included in how we communicated about the infrastructure plan, if only because it would prevent them from saying that the White House had excluded them from the conversation.

Here we've arrived at our second step in audience engagement. Once you've identified your audience, the second principle of connecting with them is to use what you know to figure out how best to appeal to their priorities.

Because the bill was so detailed, some might think a good route to engagement with reluctant members of Congress would be for me to explain every aspect of the legislation that would create specific benefits in districts controlled by the bill's opponents. That way, each of them could go back to their voters and explain their concrete reasons for voting in favor of the bill. Simple, right? Show your audience you respect them as capable of comprehending the sometimes complex language of a congressional bill, pinpointing the information that is relevant to them and their constituents. Getting a new bridge, or better ventilation in your district's schools, could be sold to voters in apolitical terms, after all. If I took the time to work with the communications and legislative teams to tailor pitches to every congressperson who was on the fence, that effort might also demonstrate how much the Biden administration cared about the details of the bill, and about each district.

We did do some of that, on a very targeted basis with local media, but on the macro level, we knew it wouldn't be effective as an over-arching message from the White House. Many of those opposed to the infrastructure agreement didn't just complain that it was too expensive—they viewed the bill as yet another example of the federal government gone out of control. It included more than two thousand pages of programs and protocols. We did not want to emphasize the bill's length or complexity. So while I *could* have explained long lists of the specific benefits the bill would bring to each of the 435 congressio-nal districts, the public was likely to reject our framing that the bill was "comprehensive" and instead insist the government was biting off way, way more than it could chew. According to the opponents' logic, this would result in billions of dollars of wasteful spending, a titanic bal-looning of bureaucracy, and bridges that would remain under construc-tion because of government inefficiency and two-thousand-plus pages of oppressive regulations. As with any bill that long, there were defi-nitely proposals that had been lodged into the legislation that seemed unlikely to pass in Congress—not as many as the opponents would claim, but their specific objections to the bill were a great reason not to transform our talking points into a battle over the fine print.

Focusing on the big picture was a tactical choice rooted in a com-munications strategy. We never misled anyone about what the bill con-tained; if you wanted to read it, you were free to do so. But despite the common sense that the more information you can provide to someone you're hoping to engage, the better, showing off my knowledge of every nook and cranny of the infrastructure bill would not have been getting into the weeds. It would have been stepping into quicksand.

Instead, we went with a more emotional appeal. We stressed that the bill would help shorten commute times (who would oppose that?), rebuild the nation's many crumbling roads that could no longer withstand traffic, and make sure everyone, whether in a city or a rural community, had access to broadband internet. In the end, it worked: while we weren't able to convince every single member of Congress to support the legislation, nineteen Republicans in the Senate voted in favor of the infrastructure bill. Including Mitch McConnell. And most of those who opposed it were more than happy to take the money it provided—and even take credit for the benefits the bill delivered to their districts.

You might be surprised by what kind of incentive will help your audience engage. Whenever possible, lower the barriers to engagement.

My plan to explain to my five-year-old daughter that I was about to start a time-consuming job at the White House began with me proposing a trip to her favorite frozen yogurt shop, beloved for its many flavors of soft serve and its wide range of toppings that no sane adult would combine. As we settled on a bench outside the yogurt shop, I began my big-picture explanation of why I felt it was important for me to do the job at that particular moment, which I had written out in advance. I really thought I had the message to my target audience nailed.

"So, remember that nice man, Joe Biden, won the election to be the president, right?"

"Yep," she said between bites.

"Well, he asked me if I could help him for a little while," I explained.

"OK," she muttered. This wasn't a shy or disappointed mutter; it was the mutter of someone more interested in the gummy bears and Oreos that were spilling over the top of her cup than in what I was saying. My attempt to lower barriers to engagement was beginning to backfire. I pressed on.

"And it's going to mean sacrificing time away from you and Matthew," I continued. Her little brother was two at the time. "But it's for the country. So that means *you* are also sacrificing to help make people's lives better in the country. Does that make sense?"

My own frozen yogurt was melting in the cup as I waited for her response.

"Not really, Mom," she said.

I laughed. I had indeed identified the right audience, but despite my thoughtful attempts to craft a larger point about service and sacrifice, my attempt to lower a barrier to engagement with treats just made my daughter focused on the treats. In retrospect, it seems obvious that a five-year-old was not going to engage with the issue of Mom not being around as much when I put it in terms of patriotic abstraction. But she did enjoy her froYo.

It would be a while before I got another chance to explain to my kids what I did at work. Because of the stringent COVID restrictions, family members were not invited to visit the White House for almost the entire first year of the Biden presidency. My kids would occasionally see me on television, but they mainly experienced my job through the changes to my daily schedule, specifically what time I left for work in the morning and when I came home. (For some reason my son was under the impression that I worked at the car dealership at the end of the street.)

Finally, in November of 2021, we learned that the president would be hosting the annual Turkey Pardon, when two turkeys receive a public pardoning and are sent to live on a farm instead of becoming someone's Thanksgiving dinner. The lucky turkeys even stay in a fancy hotel downtown the night before the big family event, a tradition that goes back to the presidency of George H. W. Bush.

The morning of the pardon, I met my kids outside the White House front gates and walked with them along the long driveway that divides the building from the area called Pebble Beach, where network correspondents broadcast live. As I pointed out that area to them, I tried to explain what the reporters did. "These are the people who tell you what is happening in the news when we watch *The Today Show* in the morning." I also showed them where the president and his family lived. Then we visited my office and went down to the White House mess, a small cafeteria counter run by the Navy.

My daughter immediately spotted the soda machine. She had never seen anything like it. This wasn't just a typical machine that you would find in a fast-food restaurant, it was digitized with multiple screens of options. I took this all for granted, but to a six-year-old that machine was magic. After much consideration, she selected a Sprite, which she had never tasted before.

We sat close to the front of the crowd for the pardon of the turkeys Peanut Butter and Jelly, and even I groaned as President Biden made dad jokes like "Build back Butterball"—a reference to "Build Back Better," the ambitious proposal that would expand parental leave and the child tax credit and invest in addressing the climate crisis, the administration's major domestic policy push at that point. After that, President Biden walked around to greet the families, including ours. My normally talkative six-year-old was pretty quiet. When the president bent down to shake her hand she simply said, "Hi," in a loud voice. Matthew didn't even speak. Before we left, a member of the First Lady's team dropped off turkey-shaped cookies, which the kids inhaled on the way home.

That night, I asked my daughter what she'd liked best about visiting the White House. I wondered if she'd understood my job better after meeting the president, walking around the Rose Garden, and meeting the reporters she sees on television. She was pretty clear on her answer.

"I learned I love Sprite, and the president is really good at making cookies."

It was not what I imagined her takeaway to be. But soon after, she started telling our family and friends that she loved where I worked.

My talking points on our historic tour that day were not going to convince her that what I was doing was valuable. That her engagement involved elements I considered trivial—the White House cookies are excellent, but not going to convince me of much, policy-wise—was no reason to discount their emotional power. I could have explained to her that soda and cookies were not what she was supposed to care about. But because she now had a true connection between her happiness and Mom's office, I had something to build on if and when she needed to develop a broader understanding of why I was coming home late. Or maybe I wouldn't bother, and just let her go on thinking President Biden bakes good cookies.

Once again, common sense in communications is not as common as you think. This can be true even for adults, because presenting information straightforwardly with data and details is not always the most effective strategy. It often misses the emotional connection. A long speech, a fact sheet, or a lengthy essay is often not the most effective way to explain an issue or move people to care about it—though these tools can appeal to those already on the same side. There is a famous quote often attributed to Maya Angelou that captures this point: "People will forget what you said, people will forget what you did, but people will never forget how you made them feel."

It's always nice to have a succinct, three-step process. To recap, the three principles of strategic communications are: identify the audience, use what you know to figure out how to engage them, and lower barriers to that engagement. Still, there's no foolproof plan, as my attempt to explain patriotic duty to my daughter demonstrates.

Besides tactics that are simply misguided, there are a few other typical hurdles to audience engagement. The first, and most important, is that you may be trying to sell something that is unsellable, and no amount of spin will convince your shrewd audience that they should seriously consider what you have to say. On the White House communications team, we had a little mantra that I recited if we were asked to push something we knew was going to sound like a bad idea: "not a comms problem!" When the problem was not the language being used but a weakness of the policy or product, it didn't matter how well we sold it: the audience wasn't going to buy it. Often, the messenger gets blamed for this. That was also part of my job—being the messenger who could shoulder some of the blame.

After the initial weeks of the COVID-19 pandemic, the big question on many parents' minds was when schools would open again. As the crisis wore on, I was asked dozens of questions about this. How would we define "open"? Staggered attendance to limit the number of students and teachers in buildings at any given time? Total business as usual? During a meeting with senior advisors, we talked about how we should explain our policy. We didn't want to overpromise, and we also wanted to make clear that we had every intention of making progress. We decided to announce publicly that we were aiming to open schools for one day a week, every week.

So that's what I went out to the podium and announced. Looking back, the response was not hard to predict. Pretty much everyone—from the reporters in the room to the public on social media to even my friends on our ongoing text chain—let us know they thought this policy was absurd, the worst of all worlds. How could that possibly be our goal? Parents would need to find childcare for the other four days. There would be a significant amount of learning loss. The truth is, it was an unpredictable time and while we wanted schools to be open five days a week, we didn't know if that was going to be possible across every school district. We did not want to overpromise and underdeliver. But as a result, we appeared more like we were underpromising and preparing to underdeliver.

In the senior staff meetings that night and the next morning, we discussed our response and agreed we should focus the conversation on our most ambitious goals in terms of reopening schools. We quickly adjusted our message—responding to feedback is an important skill I'll get to in a later chapter! Our real aim was to have schools open five days a week, and we were putting in place implementation strategies through the Department of Education to get it done.

Other obstacles to audience engagement are harder to predict. Unsurprisingly, some rhetorical tricks that work in one context don't necessarily work in others. The famous "recency effect," a cognitive bias that says audiences tend to remember whatever was mentioned last (or most recently) more clearly than what came first, can be a valuable tool for getting an important message across—but it only works if you can keep your audience interested until the end of your conversation, meeting, or presentation. It may even be irrelevant in an age when so many efforts to communicate are sliced into thirty-second clips, click-bait headlines, and social media posts, and when our attention spans have adjusted a little too well to the new paradigm.

On the other hand, there's the belief that what the audience encounters first establishes the frame that can mask much of the less welcome content that follows. (A spoonful of sugar—or frozen yogurt—helps the medicine go down.) It's only with a solid understanding of your audience and their priorities that you can begin to determine which strategy will work best for you.

Still, there are some tried-and-true methods for appealing to wide audiences, or audiences you might not have time or resources to get to know very well before you have to communicate with them. The best approach to any kind of communication you might find yourself prepping for—one that both limits boredom and keeps the audience engaged even if the message isn't something they want to hear—is to think of yourself as a storyteller. We are narrative creatures, and we understand our lives through stories. Braiding emotional resonance into a story creates the maximum chance of engagement.

Take these two statements about gun violence, a topic I've tragically had to address more times than I can count:

1. Children are at risk of gun violence as soon as they leave the house, or are at school.
2. There is widespread support for changes in gun laws.

These two statements are based in fact; statistics and data can back them up. But that doesn't matter so much to someone who strongly disagrees with the notion of stronger laws to address gun violence.

So now take a look at these:

1. Every time my children walk out the door or I drop them off at school, I am afraid.
2. The public will support changes in gun laws. It's the politicians who are holding up reforms and undermining safety.

The first two statements are perfectly clear and 100 percent factual. But they are statements. The other two? Stories. They have characters, tension, and emotion; they go beyond politics. When you read them, what imagery popped into your head? Fearful parents, terrified children under their desks; maybe you remembered some of the news stories you'd seen about school shootings, or the screenshots of text messages sent between children and parents during school shootings that proliferated on social media. You might have remembered the small but palpable lack of control you feel every time your child steps out of the house. The point is, we can all relate. Which of the options do you think has the best chance of engaging someone who is on the fence about whether the United States should implement stricter gun-control laws?

In order to answer that question, you should say, Well, it depends. Is the skeptic a parent? That would be your first step to knowing your audience. Then you should think about what kind of language would work best to break through to that group. Finally, lower the barrier to entry, so that when you do try to engage, they don't slam the door on you and your Palm Pilot.

2

What If I Don't Know Enough about Venezuela?

On the importance of research, planning, practice, and scripting,
to decrease anxiety and avoid insulting famous rappers

President Biden popped by my office to find the entire press team in the
midst of our daily pre-briefing cram session.

If the task of identifying your target audience is the first step to communicating effectively, the second is figuring out what you're going to say to them. People who love binders, folders, color coding, and studying are going to like what's coming next. That's right—this chapter is about planning, research, and practice. And if you think you don't like those things, I promise preparation can be as enjoyable as any other aspect of communication. Maybe even more so. Either way it will make you a far better communicator.

In nearly every job I've had since I was twenty-three, I've needed to understand, and be able to explain, the basics of many different topics. My expertise didn't necessarily start in a certain subject, but I discovered quickly that learning as much as I could on whatever I was going to be speaking about publicly made me more effective at my job. That doesn't mean memorizing sound bites and quippy one-liners. It means that while I'm always trying to prioritize and antici-pate what will come next, reading and researching widely have long been a part of my daily routine. And in order to make that feasible, I've had to determine which topics are the most important to focus on at any given time.

When I worked as the White House press secretary, my alarm typi-cally went off just after 5:00 a.m. After chugging a cup of coffee, on my most organized days, I'd send an email to members of my team. This tactic—which I'd learned as the spokesperson for the State Department nearly ten years earlier—conveyed clear daily goals to our group. Over the years, that email became less formal, but more for personal than professional reasons: between my stint at the State Department and the White House podium, I had two kids. I didn't have time to create a beautifully polished agenda for the day, just as I no longer had the lux-ury of devouring a stack of daily newspapers over breakfast. But I knew that even thirty minutes of reading, scanning, and narrowing would help me both in my daily work and in the long term. So I'd listen to podcasts while drinking my second cup of coffee in the shower; I'd read headlines and articles on my iPad and type out thoughts on my phone while on an exercise bike in my basement, simultaneously watching *Morning Joe* and keeping my kids occupied with coloring books on the floor nearby. By the time I made it to my car, I would be calling into a morning check-in with my team. And when I pulled into the

White House employee parking lot at around 7:45 a.m., I was pretty confident that a combination of my preparation, years of experience, and gut instinct would help me predict which stories the media would continue to follow that day. I didn't exactly listen to those mindfulness apps that suggest focusing on one thing at a time, but what I lost in mindfulness I gained in crossing things off my checklist.

And then it was time to return to those early-morning emails. These missives usually took the form of a list, and a typical version had a few bullets with questions or topics along these lines:

COVID:
- timeline for kids' vaccine
- latest on WH masking policy
- plans for next COVID briefing by health experts

RUSSIA:
- latest on discussions w/ Ukraine and Europeans
- update on deliveries of weapons
- response to Zelensky requests

ECONOMY:
- expectations for GDP data
- latest on child tax credit discussions
- Manchin conversations

Because you can't bring a cell phone into the Oval Office, or into the suite of national security offices, I often transferred the list, in Sharpie, from email to a note card that I carried to morning meetings. This note card became the driver for my day, reminding me of key priorities. The list evolved as staff members added topics. By the time we started briefing prep mid-morning, we could narrow down which topics should get the most attention. Inevitably, as soon as we started moving forward on the list, a news story would break and we'd have to adjust. But it was still a foundation from which we could build and keep track of issues that might not have otherwise been at the forefront of our minds.

Once I'd narrowed down the issues I needed to focus on, I did some more targeted research, including seeking out and reading specific articles, watching news pieces, and, yes, seeing what people were saying on Twitter. The goal was to become my own version of an expert—not as expert as the "real" experts, but informed enough that I could have productive conversations with those experts.

At some point during all this, I would also have a check-in with the president, typically around 10:00 a.m. in the Oval Office. If there was nothing urgent to discuss, we would start by going through a document we called NOTD, or "News Of The Day." If he was planning on taking questions from reporters that day, he would give his feedback on the responses we'd drafted for him on the various issues he might be asked about. That was a process my team started early in the mornings so we could discuss it on our morning call, narrowing down the main topics we thought reporters would ask about and drafting short, bullet-point answers. I would review the document just before my morning meeting with senior advisors; I often read over the shoulder of one of the press assistants as they typed it up. The document needed to be printed and on the president's desk when he arrived for the day.

In turn, the president would give us updates on his discussions with members of Congress about legislation we were trying to get passed or notes on his most recent calls with foreign leaders, or information about the latest policy proposals he was considering. Most of these updates were not meant for public consumption, but understanding the full picture helped me frame what we could say to the press.

*   *   *

It can be tempting, especially if you're someone who's good at delivering presentations and speaking on your feet, to give short shrift to prep work. Being good at bullshitting is also its own skill—but not one I'll be illuminating in this book. The hard truth is, I've never encountered a successful communicator who thinks, *I did too much research.* The saying "knowledge is power" is popular for a reason.

So before going into any meeting—professional or social—I try to do some research. It may feel like a time suck, but fact-finding increases the chance of a productive interaction and may save you a lot of cringing.

In 2016, when I was White House communications director, I invited my mom to be my date to a state dinner honoring Italy. The event was scheduled to take place in a large tent on the South Lawn of the White House and included musical performances, with Blake Shelton and Gwen Stefani headlining. In the very limited free time I had in the days leading up to the dinner, I thought I had everything under control—I was making sure my mom knew how to get into the White House, confirming my husband could be home from work in time to take care of our daughter, and trying to find a fancy-enough outfit that would fit me less than a year after having a baby. I didn't leave myself even five minutes to glance at the seating chart for our table.

State dinners are formal events held to honor a foreign head of state. A mix of political and cultural figures always attend, and as a result the nights are a big deal, as well as an opportunity to have a little fun on the job by mingling with celebrities and international politicians. I'd been to several state dinners over the course of my career, so I figured that I'd had years of preparation for this kind of thing—I would be fine no matter whom I was sitting next to.

After I had squeezed into a long red dress and found my seat at the dinner table, I struck up a conversation with the man to my left. He looked about twenty years old, and I assumed he'd come with his own mother, who was seated next to mine. As we dug into the first course of sweet potato agnolotti with butter and sage, we started talking about politics, and other events in the world. At some point, he referred to the time he'd recently spent "in the studio."

A painter? Sculptor? A TV host? Naturally, I asked him, "So what do you do in the studio?"

Well, it turns out, he does a lot. The person sitting next to me was Chance the Rapper. As you probably know, he's a very famous musician, one of President Obama's favorites. A quick Google search would have told me that Chance is also an activist with long ties to Chicago politics through his parents: his father had been an aide to Mayor Harold Washington and later to then-senator Obama, and his mother had worked for the Illinois attorney general. He was completely gracious about my awkward question, but someone else might not have taken it as kindly.

Failing to recognize a celebrity was not a diplomatic blunder of epic proportions. That's true for most of our daily interactions. But it's still embarrassing, even unintentionally rude, and it can mean missing an opportunity to engage more deeply with an interesting person. That night it definitely would have been worth a few minutes of googling to come better prepared.

Even when it feels like you don't have the time, doing some planning and research not only helps you gather background information and avoid embarrassment; it also gives you a better foundation when you need to go deeper. Sometimes that involves seeking guidance from actual experts. As a spokesperson for the State Department and the White House, I was privileged to have access to a range of experts on extremely complicated issues. From them, I could borrow a bit of expertise for myself, gaining the crucial perspective that would allow me to distill information that would be most valuable when I had to communicate to the press and the public.

When Ukraine became a dominant issue in the White House briefing room in 2022, I had a strong base of knowledge about the country and its relationship with Russia from my time at the State Department from 2013 to 2015. That experience was tremendously helpful to, albeit different from, my job as White House press secretary. While the wider American public hadn't heard from me very often, what I said as the spokesperson for the State Department would be scrutinized by important people around the world—politicians and leaders and staff in global capitals. Foreign leaders regularly called Secretary Kerry to inquire or even complain about something I had said in a briefing (not because it was wrong, but because they had received the message we were sending, loud and clear). It required a lot of specific knowledge. My silent mantra on my first day of that job was *Don't start a war.* And that was a pretty strong motivator to stay on top of the details.

The journalists who cover the State Department don't necessarily make that easy. They sometimes asked difficult questions about obscure issues to test what I knew. Or they'd ask questions about huge, complicated topics that were difficult to answer elegantly without giving away information the department wanted to keep under wraps, for a variety of reasons. The briefings were often ninety minutes long (versus the White House briefings, which usually ran more like forty-five minutes) and the reporters in the room dictated the focus each day. You could spend forty minutes on one topic if they kept asking questions about it—so you needed to be ready to answer questions on a single topic for forty minutes.

All this is a good thing; it kept me prepared and accountable. But I still had to focus my attention on getting back up to speed on all the latest details when Russia invaded Ukraine in 2022.

I quickly realized I couldn't rely on the often fifty-plus pages of bureaucratic talking points that had been spit out of the national security inter-agency process and then dropped on my desk every day. Instead, I read everything possible about the situation, reviewed the State Department and Defense Department briefings, and closed the door to my office so that I could concentrate while typing out the top questions I thought would come up, and then form my own attempts at answers. When I was satisfied—or what passes for satisfied when you're under tremendous time pressure—I would often email a draft of my questions and answers to several senior officials, including Jake Sullivan, the national security advisor, Jon Finer, the deputy national security advisor, and Ron Klain, Biden's chief of staff. I would then incorporate their feedback into new answers. They were able to dial me down, push me further, or correct a misunderstanding before I went into the briefing room. Rephrasing their commentary in my own words also tested my knowledge. If I got stuck, it meant I still needed to talk through an issue more.

I tried not to approach any of these experts empty-handed, but with a proposal of what I thought I *could* say. The goal was to ask questions that made it clear I understood they were very busy and didn't have time to lead a Ukraine 101 seminar—that I respected their unique, deep knowledge. And while it took effort for me to narrow down the questions I needed guidance on, the process actually ended up *saving* time in the long run. It increased the likelihood that I would be able to accurately answer the questions the reporters in the room were asking, and not have to follow up after the briefing, or make an uninformed mistake and then have to spend time mopping it up. It also reduced the likelihood that I would find myself rifling through those stacks of bureaucratic pages during the briefing, wasting anxious seconds which can feel like hours when you're on-camera. If you want to succeed as a communicator, you have to think of the gaps in your knowledge as opportunities, not weaknesses. Everybody has them, but not everybody takes the time to fill them.

Realizing you've pulled off a difficult presentation or interview, sounding sharp and knowledgeable along the way, might be a moment of celebration and relief, but you should never *really* stop preparing, in one way or another. I've spent time with a lot of very busy people—business leaders, prominent journalists, and multiple presidents. Despite the unusually high demands on their schedules, something they all have in common is that they carve out time for reading, and for consuming information that may not seem to have anything to do with their jobs. When Barack Obama released his summer reading lists, or his top book recommendations for the year, a chorus of "yeah, right" could occasionally be heard from certain quarters of the internet where skeptics who doubted he had time to read contemporary literature liked to hang out. But President Obama read all those books, and many more. Taking time after a long day to sit down and read some Chinese science fiction, a novel by Jesmyn Ward, or even one of Ron Chernow's biographies was an escape, but it also oxygenated Obama's brain. There may not have been a specific moment when he consciously connected the dots between a novel he'd read two years earlier and the issue at hand, but moving beyond your own experience is an important part of developing the kind of perspective that helps with decision-making. It's also how the most effective people connect. Developing broad general knowledge gives you the flexibility to adapt to your audience on the fly, as well as the ability to naturally relate to diverse groups. And besides, have you ever recommended a book to someone who ended up really loving it? It's a unique way of understanding someone better—and that kind of communication goes both ways.

But research—whether targeted or general—is just one aspect of being ready for anything that might come your way. Jesper Sørensen, a professor at Stanford's Graduate School of Business, likes to compare the classroom to a theater, with the professor at center stage. That doesn't mean Sørensen believes students should be passive witnesses to the professor's performance, without playing a role in the discussion— quite the contrary. What he means is that if you're leading a room, you need to be aware that your effectiveness with your audience has much in common with how an actor is viewed. If that actor forgets his lines or freezes onstage, or even if he just stumbles, the audience will recognize that he's a performer going through the motions and some of the magic will be lost. They might get distracted. They might even sneak a peek at their phones. If you "break character," it sends a message to the audience that what you are delivering is not authentic. And if you're not an actor onstage, but someone whose authority might be questioned or complicated—if you're giving a sales pitch or conducting a press briefing, say—they'll feel you're just pretending, and they'll think you're trying to trick them.

That's another reason why prep is so important: when your script and delivery are fluid you won't give the impression of just acting a part. Preparation gives you the confidence to deliver a great interview, performance, talk, or presentation because it gives you the background expertise and experience to sustain that confidence.

Another thing many of the high-performing people I have worked with have in common is that, in addition to reading a lot, they write a lot. They understand that writing out their thoughts, whether for a prepared speech or a spontaneous conversation, will help them think more clearly beforehand, and they've also learned that if you can't clearly articulate your thoughts in writing, you're probably not going to be able to articulate them while speaking. Especially if you only have a few minutes before the commercial break.

This is a lesson I had to relearn when I switched from being press secretary to TV host. In my early MSNBC practice sessions, producers would upload pre-written monologues, and I struggled to get the delivery right. I would pause in weird places and miss the intended emphasis of certain words. I was speaking English, but sometimes the cadence was closer to . . . robot. It wasn't a content problem—the scripts were well researched and well written. The problem was that the phrasing wasn't natural to me and didn't sound right coming out of my mouth.

I asked some of my more experienced colleagues at the network how I could improve. A number of anchors encouraged me to write my own scripts or at least heavily edit the drafts into my own language. My earliest scripts lacked the finesse of more experienced news writers, but the process allowed me to find my voice. And reading my own scripts also revealed when I wasn't making a clear or effective argument—I knew what I was trying to say, so I could more easily rephrase it when it didn't quite work as I'd intended.

If you ever try reading something you've written aloud, you'll be amazed at how often you stumble on a line that you thought was smooth when you read it silently. Those stumbles aren't always because the wording is clunky. In fact, the wording can be eloquent, but just not the way you would normally speak. Whenever you're drafting something that will be spoken aloud, whether for a speech, a debate, a toast, a presentation, a eulogy, or a news broadcast, read it out loud while you're writing. I'd learned this trick at the State Department and White House, but in a new environment sometimes you just need a reminder that when lessons universally apply, they universally apply.

Another one of those lessons is that practice makes perfect. Let's rewind to my first briefing as White House press secretary. Though you already know how the story ends, it's important to remember how I got there: countless hours of preparation, scripting, editing, and practice. When I was preparing to start the job, about six weeks ahead of the inauguration, a former colleague, Patrick Rodenbush, helped me put together about ten mock briefings over Zoom. Dry runs aren't unusual for people who work in government. When presidential nominees for executive and judicial positions that require Senate approval are preparing to testify at their confirmation hearings, they go through several practice sessions, called moots, in which their colleagues pretend to be different members of the Senate, throwing out difficult questions. These sessions mimic the flow and feel of an actual press conference, hearing, or public presentation. (As you might suspect, they can also be kind of fun.)

In my case, I prepared a briefing book, with tabs and dividers to simulate what the real thing would look (and feel) like when I started at the White House. For a few weeks in late December, members of the incoming press team and I gathered at the Department of Commerce, often double-masked, to set up mock briefings. I even practiced walking onto the platform and stepping up to the podium in heels. I wanted no surprises when I did the real thing for the first time. We set up a big screen, where we had former reporters and former White House spokespeople Zoom in to play a range of briefing room personalities. Under Patrick's leadership, and with some helpful guidance from my friend Robert Gibbs, the former White House press secretary under President Obama, each practice briefing had a different focus, requiring me to go deep on the trickiest questions around any particular issue.

As we got closer to Inauguration Day, I switched over to the actual leather briefing book that I would be using on my first day—practicing everything from flipping through its pages to seeing how the dividers would be organized and labeled. Several former colleagues and friends continued to play generic reporter roles and tested me. They grilled me on complicated economic details. They gave me a hard time from a right-wing perspective. They asked personal questions about the president and his family. While they didn't play actual reporters, they took on the personas of specific outlets. Friends I had worked with in Democratic politics and known for years suddenly became the embodiment of Fox News. I had a few rough mock briefings in the early days; I was lured into debating with "reporters" who were spouting conspiracy theories or pushing me on hypotheticals. They asked me endless questions about what would happen if the president got COVID; I learned not to go down the rabbit hole of answering questions about his hypothetical treatment plan. They pushed me to commit to deadlines for moving past COVID, for economic recovery, for his first foreign trip. All traps to set goals and schedules that might be impossible for the administration to meet.

We also workshopped answers and talked about ways to navigate aggressive, persistent, and repetitive questioners. (Occasionally these qualities are all rolled into one person.) At times, I was too serious and stoic; at others, too jovial and silly. But over the course of these mock briefings, I was able to fine-tune my style, both because of the nuanced discussions and feedback I got from my colleagues and because I was simply practicing doing the same thing over and over again. I was able to notice when particular behaviors or aspects of my performances started feeling less like things I needed to do consciously, or keep in mind, and more like natural expressions of myself in the role of White House press secretary.

After the January 6 attack on the Capitol building, we had to go back to working from home. Unable to continue practicing at a podium in the Department of Commerce, I stacked books on a tray in my house and leaned my binder on top. I set my computer on another stack of books on a table so that I could stand while answering questions during mock briefings over Zoom, to continue modeling what it would look and feel like on my first day. By the time my first briefing came around, I felt comfortable flipping through the briefing book and I knew where every tab, label, and sub-label was located, from "Climate" to "Yemen."

The night before the briefing, I was pacing around my kitchen in sweat pants and a worn-out T-shirt from the 2012 Democratic convention. Joe Biden would be sworn in the next morning, and just a few hours later I was scheduled to hold the new administration's first press briefing. My brain was filled with details about the dozens of executive orders planned for day one, including undoing the previous administration's travel ban against individuals from Islamic countries and rejoining both the World Health Organization and the Paris Climate Agreement. I was going over notes on COVID and school openings when, suddenly—shit!—an issue popped into my head that I felt unprepared to address. I started pacing faster.

Concerned by my loud footsteps, my husband, Greg, who is characteristically calm (except during a Cincinnati Bengals game), popped into the kitchen to check on me.

"Everything OK in here?" he asked.

"What if I don't know enough about Venezuela?!" I may have yelled.

As soon as I said it out loud, I realized how ridiculous it sounded. Greg assured me that the odds of someone in the press corps raising the topic of Venezuela on Biden's Inauguration Day were pretty low. What I needed to do was focus on what I *did* know and how to communicate what was important to the administration from the start.

If you ever watch a spokesperson, an anchor, or a performer and think to yourself, *Wow, that looks easy*, it isn't. Anyone who comes across as "a natural" has been studying, writing, and practicing behind the scenes. That background effort is what makes them seem relaxed in the foreground. Their goal is to replace "feeling nervous" with "feeling prepared."

Recalling her own struggles with stage fright before a big presentation, the psychologist Kelly McGonigal explains: "When I start to feel anxious now, I will say to myself, *my heart is in it*, which is a kind of a mindset reset. You know, I can feel my heart pounding maybe, or I feel other stuff happening in my body. And saying my heart is in it is a way of embracing that one of the reasons I have anxiety is not because my nervous system is broken, or I'm a person who just can't face life. I have anxiety in moments that matter where I recognize that something is at stake, and I want to contribute, or I want to do my best." Sometimes when I was about to give an important briefing during my time in government or conduct an interview on MSNBC, I was reminded of the moments when, even after I'd been swimming competitively for years, I stood on the edge of the pool at a meet and didn't want to jump in, afraid of how cold the water would be, or whether I'd be able to go faster than my competitors. Once I made the leap, however—after a brief cold-water shock to the system—everything was fine, and I was present in the moment. I could focus on the race, with years of training, drills, and practice behind my performance. Now, if I'm properly prepared, after that first splash, most of the fear vanishes. If you have a sense of what to say, and how to respond, a great amount of anxiety can evaporate more quickly than you might imagine.

After Greg reassured me that I probably wouldn't be asked about Venezuela at my first press briefing, he went to bed, and I sat down at the table to review my notes some more. I practiced the beginning of my remarks out loud to my attentive kitchen appliances, reminding myself of a crucial principle of public speaking: as with swimming, the beginning is always the hardest part. The key is getting comfortable with how you're going to start—with the very first sentence. After that, you're on a roll.

When I finally went to sleep that night, I was still nervous, but I felt ready. My heart was in it. At the briefing, I took questions, and there were many. Some were hard. But as Greg predicted, *none* of them involved Venezuela.

Few people are going to have the opportunity (or the need) to rehearse for a big presentation or speech to the extent that I did, but for anything that involves public speaking, your own "simulation" should include a physical dimension—even if your practice session involves you speaking into your hairbrush while your dog looks on from the living room sofa. If you're especially nervous about an upcoming meeting or interview, it helps to practice. If you're planning on standing during your exchange, practice while standing; the same goes if you're going to be sitting, be it at a desk, side by side on a plane, in a car, or in a chair backed up against a conference room wall if you don't yet have a seat at that table. If you have a child in elementary school and expect a tough parent-teacher conference, you *could* prepare by sitting in a chair meant for someone less than four feet tall. But that level of prepping is a bit extreme, even for me.

Practice also means studying performances in the same genre as the one you hope to give. Besides reading some of the memoirs of previous press secretaries and studying transcripts from their more notable press conferences, I watched footage of press briefings to examine how my predecessors had delivered different kinds of news. Presidents have chosen aides with experience in journalism since at least Lincoln—one of Lincoln's private secretaries edited and owned a newspaper, and the first president to give an interview to the press was his successor, Andrew Johnson—but the first official White House press secretary was George Akerson, under President Hoover. The practice of hosting daily briefings between an aide and reporters dates to Woodrow Wilson's administration—Wilson also gave the first White House press conference, though of course it wasn't televised. John F. Kennedy held the first live televised news conference in 1961, but TV cameras weren't allowed into the daily briefings until President Clinton's press secretary, Mike McCurry, initiated the practice.

I still consider McCurry a model for the job—since the advent of recording technologies that allow us to see past press secretaries in action, of course—because his strong command of the issues made him appear relaxed and almost always in control. Studying many different press secretaries' cadences and rhythms, and seeing how things flowed when a session was going well, and when it wasn't, was extremely valuable.

If you don't anticipate giving a press briefing anytime soon, there are still many applications for this advice. For job interviews, research can make a huge difference, and it doesn't take long. If your interviewer is a public person, read articles they've written, or articles about them. Check out what they've said on social media platforms. Write down a few facts that might be useful in conversation: Where did they grow up? Where did they go to school? Are there any issues or topics they seem to care most about on their social media platforms? While I'm not suggesting you go into an interview and regurgitate this information—which will make you seem weird at best—it will allow you to be agile in your conversation and show that you were appropriately curious and interested in your interlocutor. That alone is an effective form of communicating.

Once you've gotten a general sense of your interviewer, broaden your research and read some articles about the organization and company. Click around their website. Is there anything you see that you like? That you think you could improve? Do you know anyone who works there, or who may have worked there, who would be able to give you insights into the company culture? If so, call them. Too many people hesitate to ask for guidance out of fear that they might be an annoyance. My experience has been that people like to help. Just set a timer to keep the call short. If I'm asking someone for a favor, I like to give them an out after ten minutes. If they want to keep talking, they will.

Then, and this is key, write your own question-and-answer document in preparation for the interview. The format can be whatever works for you; it should be something you can glance at before the interview. For any job interview, you can be pretty sure you're going to be asked about your work history, your approach to challenges, and your passions, so prepare your talking points on those topics. You will likely be asked if you have any questions about the role, and it's never a good look to say, "Nope!" A couple of thoughtful questions will leave the hiring manager with the impression that you are proactive and well-informed about the kinds of responsibilities the job entails.

You will also likely be asked about your strengths and weaknesses. I like to ask job candidates what their "superpower" is. If you're applying for an administrative position, being organized and able to take initiative is a superpower; if you're applying for a job on a communications team, then the ability to deliver solid first drafts quickly is a superpower. As for the weakness question, it can feel like a trap. You should tailor what you say to the job; if your true, genuine weakness is that you're bad with deadlines, you probably shouldn't apply for a job editing breaking news stories. But if your weakness is obsessing over getting things right on the job, you might be able to turn that into a great strength as a breaking news journalist, which is the kind of job where accuracy can make the difference between success and an international misunderstanding that leads to a media frenzy. You will almost certainly be asked to walk through your work history and go into greater detail on the bullets on your résumé, so write down any important points that didn't fit on the original documents in advance. Come up with a short, cohesive story about yourself and your experience that you want to tell a future employer. Through that process you will find ways to more effectively talk about your experience. For example, if you left a job after less than a year—either by your choice or not—think about how you want to tell that story. When I left my job in government and began applying for roles in the private sector, I'd say in interviews that I learned so much in government and politics about how to work quickly on deadlines, but I wanted to experience working at an organization that has different priorities. Similarly, when I left my job at a consulting firm I was prepared to explain why: working there had shown me that I wanted to be inside a company, or organization, side by side with the leadership and the team, instead of on the outside offering advice; I hadn't realized I would miss having a direct impact on discussions in the workplace until I'd left government and experienced another side of things. The point is to frame your leaving as about learning and growing, because sometimes the framing is as important as the facts. Figure out how to describe your path to growth, or your role in taking on projects that no one else wanted to do. Your story tells the interviewer about your résumé, but also about your character. And the key is remembering that preparation is what makes you agile and flexible. So put down your notes and be in the moment. That's why you prepared.

3

That's Not Credible!

On giving and receiving feedback gracefully, tactfully,
and without disrupting international peace agreements

Feedback from President Obama can include his telling you that you
have something stuck in your hair.

If preparation is a lifelong process, so is improvement. Any successful communication strategy benefits from asking for, and incorporating, feedback. This doesn't need to come from people with high-level degrees or high-level security clearances. Your sources may be friends from college or a neighbor who has raised three kids of his own. But whether you're looking for advice on dealing with your toddler who is in a constant state of temper tantrum, trying to understand if you should take the questionable advice a higher-up has offered you, or even telling a cabinet official that they said something wrong that might have huge repercussions, learning how to give and seek feedback will make you a stronger communicator.

Telling someone how they can improve, or being told that you made a mistake, is always tough. I've struggled with seeking and receiving criticism throughout my adult life, both professionally and personally. Early on in my career I never sought feedback even though—or because—I was young and knew I could have been handling my job better. The fast-paced, survival-of-the-fittest environment of a political campaign provided a convenient rationalization for not pursuing even a short conversation about what I was doing well and what I might do better. And when I was a young White House press staffer during the first term of the Obama administration, I didn't take the initiative to ask my bosses for feedback. Though I was surrounded by some of the best communicators in politics, I just plowed through every day like I knew what I was doing. There can be some benefit to that approach— sometimes the way you learn to fly is by being kicked out of the nest— but the main reason I didn't ask for feedback was a fear of exposure, and the embarrassment that would surely follow. After all, why give someone around me a chance to think about my weaknesses? Much better to keep my head down and try to figure things out on my own, and keep my fingers crossed that I didn't blow it along the way.

It's probably always easier to give constructive criticism than to receive it—but it was also difficult to learn how I, as a young, relatively inexperienced staffer, could possibly explain to any of the intimidatingly senior bosses I've had over the years that they could be doing better, and I was going to tell them how.

I was twenty-six years old and working for Representative Joe Crowley on Capitol Hill when I got a call out of the blue from my former boss Bill Burton. I'd worked with Bill when he was a regional press secretary on the Kerry campaign, and in 2005 he became communications director at the Democratic Congressional Campaign Committee. His pitch was that I should leave my job with Joe Crowley and come work for him as a regional press secretary. I leapt at the chance both to work with Bill and also to be a part of the effort to win back the House. On my first day, Bill introduced me to Rahm Emanuel, who was then the chairman of the Democratic Congressional Campaign Committee.

Rahm has a reputation for being both hard-charging and brutally direct. I was warned that he would literally get in your face, stick the nub of his finger (lost after cutting himself in a meat-grinding accident) inches from your forehead. This only added to the legend of his toughness. I was also told that it sometimes seemed there wasn't a sentence he uttered that didn't include at least one variation of the f-word. Our first encounter wasn't exactly a warm one.

"Nice to meet you," I said after Bill introduced us.

"This is probably the closest we will ever get," Rahm responded.

As it turned out, he was wrong. My job was to work directly with congressional campaigns in the Northeast on their press strategy and provide Rahm with updates. That year a number of the most competitive congressional races were in that region: Kirsten Gillibrand was running for Congress in upstate New York, Chris Murphy and Joe Courtney were on the ballot in Connecticut, and there were a couple of crucial races in the Philadelphia suburbs. I ended up traveling with Rahm a lot over the next few months, and I quickly adapted to his expletive-laden sense of humor. I laughed at his jokes and would occasionally make my own, more demure versions. Though Rahm was still intimidating, slowly we started to develop a rapport. He would bark orders at me, on a few occasions even literally jumping on my desk while pointing at me and shouting, and I would do my best to execute them.

It wasn't necessarily how I imagined office life would be. But I learned that working for direct people is something I enjoyed and, in fact, preferred: You always knew where you stood with Rahm, and that builds trust. Which goes both ways.

One day in 2006 Rahm instructed me to call Jackie Calmes, a political reporter for the *New York Times*, and pitch her a story about a trend in the political races in the Northeast. I scribbled down what he said on a notepad and left his office to make the call, with a quick stop at the ladies' room first. A few minutes later, I called Jackie and was stunned to discover that Rahm had beaten me to the pitch.

It was embarrassing. I was still proving myself to political reporters at the time, and being preempted by my boss made me look disorganized or left out of the loop.

As soon as I hung up the phone, I was uncharacteristically fuming. I marched into Rahm's office. "Either you are the spokesperson, or I am," I said. "You decide and let me know."

The minute the words came out of my mouth, I worried I'd made a huge mistake. I'd always thought that keeping my cool was the best approach at work, and I'd just lost it on my boss.

Rahm was slightly startled, but without missing a beat, he nodded and said, "Well, OK."

The interaction had a surprising, confidence-building effect. It wasn't that I planned to yell at my boss on a regular basis—not every boss wants to be challenged, and I am definitely not recommending that everyone march from their cubicles to give the higher-ups a piece of their minds. But losing my cool in that moment led to a breakthrough in our relationship. He was a hot-tempered person, and my confronting him showed I wasn't scared of that—I could engage on his terms if necessary. (To a certain extent: I did not intend to ever climb on anyone's desk.) My pushback changed our dynamic for the better.

When working for direct people, being direct about your own point of view can earn you respect. Being a "yes-man" doesn't make you a valuable advisor. Figuring out when and how to provide the most candid and direct advice in the format and tone that works for your boss is what will make them look to you in a meeting and rely even more on your counsel. Despite his status as a controversial figure in Washington, Rahm also refreshingly ignored the typical pecking order of government bureaucracy and fiercely defended and protected the people he was close to. A phone call from him—often at some odd hour when you least expected it—might start with a tirade and end with, "OK, I love you."

It took me a little longer to find my way with my next boss. I was still in my twenties when I started working on Barack Obama's presidential campaign. The then-senator from Illinois was a rising star in the Democratic Party who came to national attention after delivering a speech that brought the 2004 Democratic National Convention to its feet. I was actually backstage in the hall that night, tasked alongside speechwriter Jon Favreau with prepping John Kerry's daughters to speak at the convention the next night. I wish I could say we had both witnessed Obama's historic speech live, but instead we were backstage with the sisters as they debated about the speaking order, just as my sisters and I probably would have.

By the time I was working at the Democratic Congressional Campaign Committee with Rahm Emanuel, Obama was the most popular campaign surrogate—the politician most often asked to campaign for other Democrats. A lot of us already believed he would be the next president of the United States. The first time I met him was months after I started working on the campaign and I'd been dispatched from Chicago to be the press staffer at a 2007 fundraiser in Cincinnati. When I arrived, I met up with members who escorted me to the tarmac and asked me to sit in Obama's car so that we would be ready to leave when he arrived. While I waited, I wondered what I should say to this already larger-than-life figure. I thought I'd come up with a pretty good line when all of a sudden he opened the door and sat down.

"I bet you are wondering who I am and why I'm in your car?"

I felt pretty proud of myself that I spit it out. That didn't last long. Somehow, in my slightly nervous delivery, I caught the arm of my purse on the door handle and half the contents flew across the backseat and into Obama's lap. Pens, lipstick, and possibly a tampon. He may have jumped, slightly, before giving me a subtly ironic look as he helped pick up my belongings now strewn across the floor of the car. This pales in comparison to the time just a few months later when I made the poor choice of jumping over a *literal* hurdle at a campaign event, splitting my pants down the middle. I landed in a media report after Obama made an offhand comment that my pants looked "pretty X-rated."

Obama is calm and cerebral, in many ways the opposite of Rahm. He didn't typically shout orders at staff (which made it that much scarier when he even slightly raised his voice). And when a staffer made a mistake, Obama's reaction often reminded me of my mother, who simply says she's "disappointed."

Of course, dumping my purse into Obama's lap wasn't really a mistake; it was actually a good way to break the ice. My first actual mistake in this job came during the first campaign summer of 2008, when I missed a bus that was supposed to take me and a group of reporters from an event to Obama's plane. We weren't stuck discussing a breaking news story. We were playing basketball in the gym and lost track of time. I am not even a hard-core basketball player; we were just taking a little break during a multiday set of campaign events. Instead of traveling on that bus in the candidate's motorcade, as we were supposed to, we had to take taxis and got stuck in horrible traffic.

The plane didn't leave without us, but by the time we got there the Democratic nominee had been waiting an hour, mostly because he didn't want to leave the reporters stranded. I sheepishly walked up to the front of the plane to apologize, bracing to get yelled at by an understandably upset Barack Obama for the first time.

"You are normally an A student," he said, always the constitutional law professor deep down. "So I am going to let this one slide."

Sometimes you can be both inspired and intimidated by someone's public persona. The first few years I worked for Obama, from the campaign to the White House, I was nervous every single time I was expected to talk in his company. For starters, he's legitimately brilliant and uniquely thoughtful in how he approaches big challenging issues, and you often had the feeling he knew not only everything you were about to tell him but also everything you were *supposed* to be telling him but hadn't had the time or high-enough IQ to learn. He holds his cards close to his chest. While he loves a good debate or conversation, and often seeks out the quietest person in the room for their thoughts, he can be uninterested in extensive feedback, especially if it is of the bloviating variety. It wasn't my job at the time to provide him with a great deal of direct information, but I became paralyzed by the fear of saying something stupid, or inappropriate, in front of him. As a result, I would try to blend into the back of the room and hope he wouldn't ask me a question. I would even suggest others go in my place to meetings he'd be attending.

That fear was exhausting. Every day I was trying to navigate my job and daily responsibilities while also handling my insecurity and nerves about interacting with my boss. I couldn't picture myself actually having a substantive role in those meetings. I couldn't even envision what I would contribute. I believe they call this impostor syndrome.

My solution at the time was to throw myself into being a team player. I sent detailed notes to my direct bosses so that they would be prepared for meetings, and I volunteered to call back reporters on their behalf when they were busy. I didn't speak up or question much. I worked long hours and developed a reputation for being one of the more organized and calm members of the team.

But that deference didn't exactly position me as someone who could strategically drive an agenda—or who could grow into a much bigger role. Feeling stalled and worn-out, I left the White House in 2011. Seeking a path to relevance outside the Obama orbit, I started working as a consultant at a communications firm.

Because I had been a senior figure in the administration and had just left the White House, I was asked to appear on a number of cable networks to talk about the 2012 presidential campaign. I quickly realized I loved it. I enjoyed advocating for President Obama and his policies, and I also really enjoyed debating members of the Republican Party, something I'd never done before. I learned I was pretty good at it, which, combined with the fun I was having, built my confidence. I started to wonder if I might not need to hide behind the scenes all the time.

Fortunately, that wasn't just my opinion. In the winter of 2012, David Plouffe, a senior advisor in the White House and the campaign manager for Obama's first presidential campaign, asked me to rejoin the team, to travel with and advise the president on media and serve as the primary on-air spokesperson for the campaign when it picked up that summer.

Right before I started, I called Robert Gibbs, who had been the White House press secretary during the first two years of the first term, for advice. I was on the verge of freaking out about this new job. I was worried about working side by side with Jay Carney, someone whom I had long admired. I was worried that Obama saw me as an obedient junior staffer and not someone he could rely on for strategic or press advice—and given how I'd attempted to blend into the scenery last time I'd worked for him, he wouldn't be wrong to do so. I asked Gibbs how I could shift his perception and establish myself as the person who deserved to be the one briefing the president for political interviews and public engagements on the road—how I could possibly see myself as equipped to give the president feedback. Gibbs's advice has always stuck with me because it was so simple—and delivered with a hint of his trademark southern drawl.

"Act like you belong there," he said, "because you do, and at a certain point everyone else will believe it, too."

I took the advice, and while I still remember the level of intense nervousness before my first campaign trip that year, after a while it got easier. I did start to believe I belonged there. I traveled with a small group of aides, including David Plouffe and Jay Carney. Because of the Hatch Act—legislation that says the activities of the incumbent as a political candidate and the incumbent as current president must be kept separate—there were limitations on what Jay could say about the campaign. So David had an idea to do joint briefings in the press cabin on Air Force One during the campaign. As White House press secretary, Jay was responsible for covering events that happened on the official, or government, side, and I was responsible for briefing the press on the political developments on the campaign trail; I also was responsible for updating the president on press coverage of the latest attacks on him from his opponent, Mitt Romney.

Joint briefings had never been done before, so there was no rule book or set of guidelines to follow. It was sort of an on-the-fly seminar (no pun intended) on how to engage with the press. I was probably shaking during the first briefing because I wanted to prove to both the reporters and Jay that I was adding value. But learning that I was able to literally keep my balance during sudden turbulence as a gaggle of reporters thrust microphones into my face eventually dispelled some degree of my impostor syndrome. As did the fact that the "Jen and Jay Show" was kind of a hit—Jay, as the buttoned-up government spokesperson, would say something like "That's correct; they're considering those sanctions," and then I'd chime in with, "Mitt Romney is a terrible person who wants to kill kittens!" Well, no, but I was proud of my dig at Romney that "the only person who has offended Europe more is probably Chevy Chase" (a reference to the movie *National Lampoon's European Vacation*).

Over time, my understanding of what worked for Obama and what didn't grew. The president was rarely flustered or visibly distressed by attacks; instead, he simply took in the information you gave him and then asked a few follow-up questions, usually about news stories or Romney campaign ads.

When I later served as Obama's communications director in 2015, I knew I belonged there and felt a lot more comfortable than the day I emptied the contents of my purse in his lap. We would bring in one slide every week that included proposed interviews or public engagements we were recommending, and a bullet or two on the justification, which he always wanted to know, and then we'd talk through it all and make decisions rapidly. It took me a while to realize that I didn't need to be President Obama's buddy, but by then I was in my mid-thirties, married, a homeowner, and a mother. With more years of life experience under my belt, I was more confident in my role at the White House: I needed to be the person who listened and understood the president's objectives, presented information and options in a format that worked for him, and calmly and clearly pushed back when I disagreed. That was more than enough.

Feedback is often about anticipating how and even when to provide it, so when I did feel the need to speak out or disagree, I knew to come prepared with an argument I was confident in. Every now and then, these arguments shaped the news. In the days leading up to President Obama's final State of the Union address in 2016, Senator Chuck Schumer insisted that some specific language about student loans be included in the speech. This wasn't uncommon—before a State of the Union address, official and unofficial lobbying for mentions in the speech is intense, and it's impossible to satisfy everyone. Even when the ask is around policies the president supports, like lowering the cost of college, the speech can become a laundry list of policies and initiatives, which mutes the core message.

We had made a strategic decision that President Obama's final State of the Union speech would not be a policy laundry list. In fact, it wasn't going to include any new policy proposals. Instead, the president would use the speech to paint a big-picture vision of where the country was headed. Ben Rhodes and Obama's chief speechwriter, Cody Keenan, had been tasked with writing the speech, and they'd spent days crafting it directly with the president. (Not an easy job under any circumstances, but even more challenging when you're working with a writer as talented as Barack Obama.) They'd been pushing back against dozens of people both inside and outside the government who wanted their initiatives mentioned. As he writes in his excellent book *Grace*, Cody was even approached by senior officials waiting for him outside the bathroom in the days leading up to major speeches.

Still, Schumer's mention was up for debate, and a photo published on the front page of the *New York Times* the day before the speech tells the story of what happened. As I'm sitting on a couch in the Oval Office with my back to the camera, the president, Ben, and Cody are across from me. I am gesturing to make a point; Cody and the president are staring at me with looks of exhaustion, irritation, or both. (Ben is looking at his notes, but in an exhausted and irritated way.) Undeterred, I made my case (that Cody and Ben shared): if the president referred to a new policy proposal on student loans, it would dilute the power of the uplifting message we were trying to communicate. In that photo, I was telling him he needed to decide whether he wanted this to be his State of the Union speech, or Senator Schumer's. I delivered my thoughts calmly. My argument tapped into my knowledge of how the media would cover the speech. The president eventually agreed. (Sorry, Senator Schumer.)

* * *

Between my roles in the Obama administration, I got probably the most decisive lessons in giving and receiving feedback I've ever had in my career. Fresh off the "Jen and Jay Show," I started working at the State Department in February of 2013. I didn't come to the job with strong foreign policy credentials: I didn't have a master's degree, and I'd never worked at a think tank. I'm not sure I even really knew what a think tank was. So when the opportunity arose to work with Secretary of State John Kerry, I hesitated. When I once again sought his advice, Robert Gibbs agreed it was a career risk given my lack of foreign policy background. But my longtime colleague and friend Ben Rhodes convinced me that I could learn what I needed to learn to do the job and encouraged me to at least go for an interview. Everyone needs both kinds of feedback: a critic who's tough but fair, and a hype man. The trick is learning which one to listen to in each circumstance.

From the outset, I knew I'd have to work hard to prove myself as well as to establish a relationship with Secretary Kerry. Despite having worked for him on his 2004 presidential campaign, I didn't know him well, and my impression of the longtime Massachusetts senator was still tainted by caricatures from that campaign, which showed him as an out-of-touch, Ivy-educated "flip-flopper." I went into my first interview expecting him to be standoffish. It became immediately clear that the patrician portrayal could not have been more wrong. Secretary Kerry was warm, friendly, and engaged. I knew from working with his daughters on his presidential campaign that he deeply loved his kids and grandkids, as the family photos prominently featured in his office reminded me. He has an uncanny love for adventure and spoke excitedly about all the work he wanted to pursue as secretary, conveying a youthful enthusiasm about public service. He wanted to hold the first ever conference on oceans at the State Department; he wanted to see if there could be a new path forward to peace in the Middle East; he wanted to strengthen the country's relationships in Asia.

I was feeling excited about these ambitions when he brought up the elephant in the room—my lack of background in foreign policy. He said he wanted to give me a chance and advised me to study up. While he wasn't extending a formal offer, his message was pretty clear. At the end of our interview, he pulled me into a bear hug.

I went straight from that meeting to the history section of Barnes & Noble, where I loaded up on books about Syria and North Korea, often falling asleep reading them in bed with the unscientific hope that the information would enter my system through some sort of osmosis. But I also thought a lot about my conversation with Secretary Kerry, and I read up on his long career in politics and government. People who are drawn to public service want to be part of a greater good—it isn't about them as individuals, but about how they can contribute. They believe in working to improve the world, regardless of how their political party may feel this is best achieved. Learning about Secretary Kerry's background and lifelong advocacy made me realize that we shared a desire to play a small role in making a difference. Understanding how my ability to craft and effectively communicate messages on policy existed in the grand scheme of public service made me grateful to be in a position to make change happen.

I had never done a formal briefing at a government podium before arriving at the State Department in 2013, and the stakes of me messing up were pretty high, not just for my own professional future, but for the country, and maybe even the world. I couldn't fudge it with *National Lampoon* jokes. I was forced to seek feedback. After I read more than one hundred press briefings conducted by Victoria Nuland, my predecessor, I began a series of practice briefings, similar to those I did before becoming White House press secretary. Their explicit purpose was to give me the opportunity to receive structured feedback, which I definitely did. Responses to my practice briefings included everything from "well, if you say that you may start a conflict," to "I wouldn't smile while you are talking about genocide," to the fact that the podium was way too high for me.

Some adjustments were obvious. No, I definitely should not have a smile plastered on my face while talking about genocide. Sometimes I asked follow-up questions including, "What can I say differently?" And "What if I said it like this?" In terms of my height and the podium, a large step covered in blue carpet to match the briefing room floor was installed before my first briefing. I found it reassuring to learn that former secretary of state Madeleine Albright carried a step with her when she traveled. Suddenly being a more petite person speaking on behalf of the United States felt cool.

Certainly, I could have done such a bad job during those State Department practice briefings that I might have been asked to leave and never return. But the goal was not to make me feel like I was on the verge of getting fired, but to help me improve. As that context became clearer, the critical feedback I received didn't seem as embarrassing as I would have expected. The seasoned State Department veterans who were throwing pitches at me were giving me an opportunity, not trying to make me slip up.

That experience prompted me to aggressively seek feedback in future jobs. Years later, if I blew it at a White House press briefing I would start our staff meeting afterward by saying something like "Well, I screwed up that answer, so let's talk about how we can fix it." Or "I'm sorry, guys; that wasn't my best. Let me know how I can help make sure reporters have what they need." Or "I owe you lunch for the cleanup you're going to have to do on that one." I wanted my team to know that I recognized when I made a mistake, and in doing so I reframed the feedback process: no one would feel awkward about breaking it to me that I'd whiffed it at the podium, because I'd opened up the forum for honest feedback by criticizing myself.

I followed the same practice when I transitioned to anchoring a TV show, starting our earliest show meetings with a self-critique about what I could have done better. I still pester Alex, the show's executive producer, and often other senior MSNBC producers about what I can do better as soon as the cameras are off, often starting with my own list. We are all works in progress, and the producers I work with usually have something to share that makes me better. They only push back when I aggressively ask for their immediate thoughts on debate or election nights, when their feedback is along the lines of "It's after midnight! We want to sleep."

But back to the State Department. To bring it full circle, one of my responsibilities as a spokesperson was to give my impressive, idealistic boss feedback on his statements and positioning. In July 2014, I traveled to Austria with Secretary Kerry, who was overseeing negotiations with Iran and five other world powers about halting Iran's progress on acquiring a nuclear weapon in exchange for economic sanctions relief. Just getting Iran to the table had been a lengthy and difficult process; high-level officials from the United States and Iran hadn't spoken for decades when the US imposed restrictions following Iran's seizure of the embassy in Tehran. That changed in 2013, when President Obama reached out to the new Iranian president, Hassan Rouhani, at the end of the annual meeting of the UN General Assembly.

At the negotiations the next year, our team—which included Wendy Sherman, the under secretary of state for political affairs and Bill Clinton's former advisor on North Korea, and dozens of nuclear experts—had been in Vienna for weeks already, banging out the details, barely sleeping, and subsisting on bad coffee and leftover croissants from the hotel breakfast buffet. Secretary Kerry was now joining them to bring their work to other chief diplomats and try to unstick some of the pieces that were holding up progress.

As spokesperson for the department, I'd been on dozens of high-wire trips with the secretary, but this one felt more consequential. I carefully picked out what I would wear each day, including my favorite St. John maroon knit suit (purchased from a consignment shop) and comfortable wedge shoes. I knew I'd be running around for the multiple eighteen-to-twenty-hour workdays that lay ahead.

A couple days after we arrived, we scheduled a press conference for Secretary Kerry to deliver an update. Every top outlet was there. The secretary was feeling positive, with good reason. He is an optimist by nature, always thinking there has to be a way to finalize a deal, and persistent to the point that he could wear down his negotiating counterparts with pages and pages of notes and the ability to function at a very high level on no sleep. Kerry loved the possibility that diplomacy offered—the possibility that you could find common ground with an adversary in order to make progress. His optimism was one of the qualities that made me love working for him.

It was also one of the hardest qualities to manage from a communications perspective. Long before we were in Vienna for the Iran negotiations, I saw this dynamic play out during a State Department trip to Japan. David Wade, Kerry's longtime chief of staff in the Senate, was traveling with us, and he knew the secretary better than almost anyone. David had acted as spokesperson and later as chief of staff in Kerry's Senate office as well as on the campaign when he ran for president. On that trip David and I watched the press conference from seats in the front row and nodded along . . . until the secretary was asked what kind of support the United States was prepared to provide if China further threatened Japan. The secretary's answer was forceful—and not exactly in line with the public US military policy.

Immediately, I could feel David grow tense next to me. I had registered the secretary's overstatement, too, and thought to myself that I would have to call my hype man, Ben Rhodes, who was one of the president's top communications advisors on national security at the time, to give him a heads-up. Together, we'd figure out how to walk this back with the press.

As soon as the press conference ended, David and I joined Secretary Kerry. The secretary was in a great mood—he thought he was done for the day. Hesitant to burst his bubble, I was ready to get to work behind the scenes, calling the White House and issuing a qualifying statement to the traveling press. Not David.

"Sir, you just made a huge mistake up there," he said. "What were you thinking?"

Wow, I thought, *that was direct.*

"That is not the policy of the president or the administration. You left the impression that we're going to use military force if there is a conflict between Japan and China," David continued. "That was a huge mistake," he repeated.

I sat quietly and just watched. Secretary Kerry didn't yell at David or get defensive. He simply gave us the nod to reach out to the White House and make sure the position of the United States was clear. Despite David's aggressive tone, or maybe because of it, Kerry recognized immediately that we needed to clarify his public statements.

In the van to the hotel that night, I reflected on how I'd been providing feedback to the secretary. My approach was gentle, and I tended to underplay any criticisms, mostly because of the same insecurities about being too inexperienced to advise someone like John Kerry, whom I respected so much. In this situation, I probably would have said something like "Well, that isn't *exactly* what we've been saying publicly, so we're going to have to just smooth it out a little bit. But it's not a problem!"

Seeing David in action, I realized it was time to change tack. Secretary Kerry was no shrinking violet—the man has three Purple Hearts! Between people who trust each other, being direct is not disrespectful. To be effective at my job, I had to be able to tell people exactly what they needed to know as quickly as I could. There were times that required a gentler approach, but advising someone is not the same as appeasing them.

Back at the Iran negotiations in Vienna, I sensed a potential problem as we were preparing for the press conference: if the secretary painted too rosy a picture, it could set the wrong expectation publicly and potentially lessen the leverage our team needed behind the scenes to complete their work.

Up against the press conference start time, the secretary gathered his notes and headed for the door, planning to tell the world that we were close to a deal when I knew we were not. I knew I needed to stop him, so I ran after him into the hall.

"That's not credible," I called out, my voice rising. "You can't say that. It's not credible!"

In the movie version of this scene, everyone in earshot—the other European delegations and reporters camped out at the hotel—would have snapped their necks to see who was standing up to the nation's top diplomat. And they would have seen 6'4" Kerry towering over 5'3" me. And like in a movie, time stood still.

But it worked. Secretary Kerry listened to me. He reined in his confidence and gave a measured press conference about the status of the negotiations.

"As I have said, and I repeat, there has been tangible progress on key issues, and we had extensive conversations in which we moved on certain things," he stated. "However, there are also very real gaps on other key issues. And what we are trying to do is find a way for Iran to have an exclusively peaceful nuclear program, while giving the world all the assurances required to know that Iran is not seeking a nuclear weapon."

More than once, an ambassador or high-level member of the State Department would comment on my level of brusqueness with the secretary during prep. But I had learned that was the best way to get his attention. Still, I didn't ever take things too far. Secretary Kerry had much more formal and informal authority than I did. But his indefatigable optimism made me want to soften my criticisms and offer a way to look on the bright side; it's hard to tell someone who's that hopeful that they shouldn't be. Over time, I compromised by often posing my feedback to Kerry's practice answers in the form of a question, like "If you say that, reporters will write that you're more confident that there will be direct negotiations between Israel and Palestine. Is that what you want?" or "If you describe the meeting in that tone, you will be criticized for being warm toward a country with a weak human rights record. Are you comfortable with that?" By presenting my feedback in question form, I was reinforcing our roles, while still asserting myself and my expertise.

There were many more trips to Vienna before a final deal was struck a year later on July 14, 2015. On that day, I was not in Austria prepping the secretary for a press conference. I was in a hospital room in Washington, DC, with my one-day-old daughter. When President Obama called me on July 13 to congratulate me on Vivi's arrival, I thanked him for checking in. I had returned to the White House as the communications director three months earlier. My husband was videotaping the conversation knowing that we would one day want to show it to our daughter. On later viewings, I could hear the president chuckling in the background as I quickly moved from my joy at being a new mom to asking him about the status of the Iran nuclear deal. My last day at work had been three days before my daughter was born, and I knew the deal was getting close. It had been something I'd worked on for nearly two years—traveling with Kerry and other negotiators, helping to communicate around highly sensitive stages of the deal, orchestrating private and sometimes secret meetings. It may sound funny, but with all the relief of holding a beautiful newborn in my arms, I still wanted to know what was happening with the Iran deal. When you're working so long on these initiatives, you become personally invested in them. You want that work to pay off not just for yourself, but for the country, and even the world.

"Don't worry about that right now," the president said. "But we are going to get it done."

The next day I watched on television as my former boss Secretary Kerry took to the podium in Vienna to announce that the United States, its partners in the EU, and Iran had "taken measurable steps away from the prospect of nuclear proliferation, towards transparency and cooperation."

I wish the story ended there. But before my daughter turned three, then-president Trump announced that he was unilaterally withdrawing from the Iran nuclear deal. Since then, Iran has continued to enrich uranium. How much? We don't know, because in June 2022 Iran removed the IAEA monitoring system that was installed after the 2015 accord. It makes me wish some of Trump's advisors had been less afraid of giving him tough feedback.

One of the most important lessons about giving and receiving criticism is to be judicious. Just as you shouldn't indiscriminately criticize the people in your life for every little thing they do, even under the guise of "helping them improve" (your sister doesn't need to learn to chop onions or load the dishwasher "the right way"), you should learn to take feedback with a grain of salt. You can't accept every piece of advice you get; a lot of it is contradictory anyway, as the dream team of Robert Gibbs and Ben Rhodes demonstrated earlier in this chapter. When you're considering whether and how much to listen to someone in your life, you have to think about their motivations for giving you the particular advice they've given: they might be competitive with you, or they might have had a tangential but ultimately unrelated experience that is clouding their perspective on *your* problem, or they might just be wrong. You also have to think about whether they've been right about the kind of thing they're advising you about in the past—do they have the experience or expertise necessary to gain your trust on this issue? Don't seek advice only from people who are going to tell you what you want to hear, like Donald Trump picking his lawyers. But also don't privilege the most negative commentary just because it can seem like the harshest critique is the truest.

Given how long I had wanted the White House press secretary job, it sometimes surprises people when I say I only ever planned to stay in it for a year. It's important to know that a year or less was what was proposed by the Biden team. But by the time I was offered the position, I had already worked for eight years in an administration, had two kids, was exploring other career paths, and had forced myself to move on from public service. I hadn't even been thinking seriously about working in government again. But I knew that taking on this role would allow me to contribute to a new administration at a pivotal moment in American history following the historically damaging presidency of Donald Trump.

I also knew from experience that a senior role in the White House consumed a lot of time, as well as mental and physical energy, and was particularly hard on a working mom. A short stint would allow me to put in 100 percent effort for the time I was there. I also loved the idea of helping to prepare the next generation of front-and-center spokespeople. Pushing some of the super talented members of the press team to grow into bigger roles ended up being one of my favorite parts of the job, particularly because they rose to the occasion, and then some.

But even for a shorter time period it involved a lot of negotiations and sacrifices, by me and by the people I care about most to make it all work. Before I accepted the job, Greg and I had a long conversation about how we could manage a shift in our household roles. You may remember my multitasking morning routine; that was thanks to Greg, who took our kids to two different schools every morning. He wrapped up bedtime if I had to be on calls after hours. He took them to birthday parties on the weekends when I was at work, and he even navigated my two COVID quarantines. I did everything I could to be present for my family, from scheduling our Friday pizza nights to spending the early waking hours with the kids, but Greg's taking on the morning routine and being prepared to jump in when, at the last minute, I couldn't be there—his flexibility made it possible for me to work at the White House with two little kids. Greg would say that year made him closer to our kids. It definitely forced our family into an equal balance of parenting, which makes for a more powerful partnership. There are all sorts of overused phrases to describe how it can be possible for two working parents to keep everything afloat. But for me it can be summed up with compromise and acceptance. Before I joined the Biden administration, Greg had been working around the clock on the Senate campaign for his then-boss Congressman Joe Kennedy. He worked longer hours, and his job took him up to Massachusetts for weeks before the primary election. For the past few years we had prioritized his career while I tried to balance professional obligations with the needs of our growing family. It worked for us, and because it did, it was easier for the roles to be reversed when I was offered what can really be described as my dream job. And it also made it easier for me to say goodbye when the time came. As I began to think about leaving, I started getting calls from people who were interested in talking about what I wanted to do next. I'd been appearing on television for over ten years and I'd worked at CNN as a contributor (this is not as fancy as it sounds—there are about 150 contributors at any time, and you're mostly there in the "talking head" role). So I started having coffee with people in the media industry. Sometimes they reached out to chat; other times it was me who initiated things, in an effort to get their advice. When it came time to talk about "what was next," I needed to say it out loud. Even if it's embarrassing, you have to talk about your goals if you want people to help you achieve them. Or if a goal is really impossible, saying it out loud can help you begin to accept that.

Some people were very encouraging and others far more skeptical. During one particular coffee with a person I respected in the industry, the reaction was a little stinging.

"I want to be an anchor," I said. "I really want to see if I can do this full-time."

She paused and considered what to say in response. "The thing is," she began, "because you're so . . . kind of . . . buttoned-up at the briefings, and you have this very steady, professional presentation, people don't see your personality.

"You're going to be hard for people to relate to," she continued, "so I don't really know how you could do it full-time."

I won't lie; this felt pretty bruising in the moment. Someone I respected was telling me this aspiration I had only recently started sharing wasn't possible.

But I didn't give up. As I took more meetings, I began getting a range of advice, and a range of encouragement. I did think about her feedback again and again, but I realized she wasn't telling me it was impossible (as I'd heard initially). She was warning me about a particular challenge I might face if I decided to take this leap. It was a reminder about both the importance of learning how to seek feedback and learning how to apply it. I understood that people knew me because of my role at the White House podium. Did I think I was always buttoned-up there? Not exactly, but I was still speaking on behalf of the US government, and that does require a certain level of . . . buttoning. But when I think back on all the meetings I had as I was considering my move away from the White House, that's the conversation that sticks with me the most. Now I know her feedback was not actually crushing; it was freeing, because it was telling me to tap into all the facets of who I am.

4

If You Can't Say Anything Nice, You Still Have to Say Something

On having tough conversations with your family, your colleagues, and Joe Biden

While some presidents prefer a more formal seating arrangement in the Oval Office, President Biden often encourages staffers to pull up a chair at his desk.

I first interviewed for the White House press secretary job when I had absolutely no business becoming the White House press secretary. When my boss, Robert Gibbs, announced he was leaving the job in early 2011, halfway through President Obama's first term, I was thirty-two years old and working as the deputy communications director for about a year after being promoted from deputy press secretary. I had been in politics for almost my entire adult life—but my adult life had not been that long. Still, after rounds of interviews with David Axelrod, who was senior advisor to Obama at the time, and the president's chief of staff, an internal process narrowed the field to me and the vice president's communications director, Jay Carney. We were each called in to meet with President Obama.

I was both eager to prove myself and terrified, worried I couldn't really prove myself. I barely slept the night before the meeting. In my head, I went over (and over, and over) the questions I might be asked, and tried to come up with ideas for what I thought we could do differently with the role. It felt a little ridiculous to be making those kinds of suggestions to President Obama, but I wanted to do my best in the interview, even if on some level I knew I wasn't getting the job. I wanted to demonstrate, if nothing else, that I could do the job one day.

The next morning, the president greeted me in the Oval Office for our one-on-one. We talked for about an hour, and when I walked out I felt a sense of relief. *I held my own . . .* , I thought, *but Jay Carney will get this job.* To be frank, I hoped Jay would get the job. At that point, I'd only done a handful of TV interviews and didn't feel ready for such a high-profile, high-stakes position. Meanwhile, Jay had more than twenty years of experience in journalism, including as the Washington bureau chief of *Time* magazine, and had been a frequent TV commentator.

A few days after the interview, David Axelrod, President Obama's longtime messaging guru, told me that, as I'd expected, they were going with Jay. But David also told me that the president had enjoyed our conversation; he hoped that I would stay on in my role as deputy communications director and encouraged David to find ways for me to grow including attending more meetings and doing more TV interviews. The extra step David took to tell me the news personally, and offer some encouragement along with it, went a long way to soften my (contained) disappointment. I was inspired to learn and grow more. I left the brief conversation hoping this wouldn't be the last time I would be considered for the job, especially if Obama won another term.

Three years later, the White House press secretary job opened up again, and I was in a very different place. While it had been pretty clear that Jay had been the right person for the role in 2011, this time around there was an expectation among the nerdy Beltway crowd that when the job opened I would be seriously considered. I also knew by then that I *could* do the job. After a brief stint in the private sector in 2011 when I left the White House due to pure exhaustion (more on that later), I came back to politics in 2012 to spend another campaign season with President Obama as the traveling press secretary for the reelection campaign, during which time I learned, grew, and maybe even charmed audiences as part of the "Jen and Jay Show" on the plane. For over a year since, I had been the spokesperson at the State Department, conducting regular sixty-to-ninety-minute briefings on a range of challenging national security issues.

The internal selection process was more nebulous this time, and from the beginning something felt different. The White House reached out to me about the job, but they didn't want to announce Jay was leaving until they decided on his successor, which made sense. Maybe, I thought, since they'd known me for years, they didn't need to do another lengthy interview process with me? At one point, I had a version of an interview with two senior advisors where the stated purpose of the meeting was to "catch up." I knew them pretty well already, but I couldn't tell if it was a real interview or just an obligatory chat so that they could say they met with multiple candidates. So at some point I said directly, "I feel like I should say I really want this job."

Clear, confident, and straightforward, but without overstepping any boundaries—qualities you'd want in a press secretary, right? In retrospect, I can see how all the background chatter got into my head: I really wanted the job, so when I heard that other people thought I would have a good shot at it when Jay left I started to believe I was made for the role.

After my series of sort-of-interviews, I waited for word that I would meet with President Obama, like last time. Then one morning, I got a call from Ben Rhodes, a speechwriter and deputy national security advisor. Now, you may be thinking, *What is the deputy national security advisor about to tell you about the press secretary job?* Well, Ben was my good friend, and he knew how much I wanted this job and how little I knew about where I stood. And that morning, he happened to find a draft statement on the photocopier announcing that Josh Earnest, the principal deputy press secretary, would get the job.

Yes, on the photocopier.

Looking back, it was clear that Josh had the inside track. He was smart and well-respected by both the press corps and the president and his colleagues (including me), and he regularly filled in doing press briefings for Jay. He was excellent at it. I was disappointed, personally, but what was more disappointing was the way I found out. I had no idea a decision had been made, or that the White House was about to announce it. When Ben realized that the plan was for the president to go out that day to the White House briefing room and announce the news himself, he called me immediately.

Ben was sympathetic, but he didn't beat around the bush. He said something along the lines of "I'm sorry. I know you really wanted this job, but they're about to announce it's going to Josh, and I wanted you to know first." Ben understood how important this was to me, and didn't want me to hear the news on, well, the news. There were also practical considerations: Ben knew I would be asked about the job at my own State Department briefing later that day (which I was) and that I would have to deal with the inevitable commentary that would accompany the decision. I couldn't express shock in public; I needed to be emotionally prepared.

Ben wasn't the decider, and he wasn't even supposed to tell me. But as my friend, he knew that hearing the bad news directly would be far less painful than hearing it with everyone else at the press briefing. And he was right: This time around, I did not feel relief. I was upset and embarrassed. It was a rejection on two levels: first because I didn't get the job, and second because none of the people I had worked for, and looked up to, and spent sleepless nights toiling beside on the original campaign and then for five years after had reached out to me with the news. At Ben's urging, one senior White House staffer did eventually call me, moments before the planned announcement, just to officially tell me I didn't get the job. But if Ben hadn't chanced upon the statement on the copier, it's likely I would have learned about it from the media. I'd given so much of myself and my energy to this team, and at the time I felt pretty let down that I didn't seem to merit more consideration in how the news was delivered.

All of this collectively stung, but it also became a case study for me in how *not* to handle a difficult conversation. A brief and to-the-point call to convey the news, ideally with enough time to process before it is made public, from one of the people making the decision would have been a far better strategy for maintaining trust and morale. It would have been difficult for me to hear in the moment, but appreciated soon after, particularly because we all had to keep working together. Outreach from people who knew I was bound to be disappointed by the decision would have softened the blow. To his credit, my boss at the time, Secretary Kerry, called me that day. "I heard you didn't get a job you wanted," he said. "I know that must be disappointing, but I am happy that means I still get to work with you every day." One thing that was particularly powerful about that call was that he knew it might be awkward, yet he did it right away. He didn't wait until we ran into each other; he knew I needed to hear from someone who valued me and my work. He was doing what great communicators do, which is putting himself in my shoes.

As I battled through my own press briefing at the State Department that day, the majority of the discussion was about foreign policy, as it always was. But I did get a question about the White House announcement. I was happy for Josh, and happy to say so, but it was still difficult to perform through all my complicated feelings, though that was a key aspect of my job. After work I hurried home, where I drank too many glasses of wine, cried a little, and wondered if I could find a way to hide from those colleagues. I went to sleep hoping I'd feel better in the morning.

I felt better when I woke up, but once I had a cup of coffee, the reality of the situation returned. In a few days I was set to embark on a trip with Secretary Kerry and President Obama, which meant I would have to face not only him but also all those senior aides involved in the staffing process. I wanted to flake on the trip. Was it possible to contract a severe case of food poisoning between now and then?

Instead of booking a table at the worst restaurant in DC, I called my mom. My mother is a therapist, as well as an incredibly warm, empathetic, never-met-a-stranger kind of person. She knew I was disappointed about not getting the job and that I felt let down by people I'd previously looked up to. I told her I worried that traveling with them was going to be awkward, but she didn't let me wallow in my anxieties.

"It takes two people to make things awkward," she told me. "So if you hold your head high, it won't be."

This was a great suggestion. At the start of the trip, I went out of my way to say hi to everyone on the team and to seek out the president to say hello. My mother's advice, as usual, was spot-on: because I didn't show that I felt rejected no one treated me any differently. As the trip wore on, projecting competence and ease made me more feel more competent and at ease. And of course all these people, especially the president, had other things to worry about. They weren't judging me or feeling sorry for me at all. They had moved on.

While part of me still felt angry and disappointed about the way the process was handled, an important part of having difficult conversations is receiving bad news gracefully. You have to know when to move forward and learn from what happened, in one way or another. For me, that meant lowering the pedestal I'd put many people on—it was unfairly high to begin with—and keeping my cool in public. I could have stomped my feet and complained to my colleagues about the process, or I could have vowed never to work at the White House again. But that would hurt me more than anyone else. Besides, I was still young. Although I had no idea the country was about to turn into a political roller coaster for the next few years and I didn't know if I'd ever get the shot to prove myself as White House press secretary, of course I eventually did get another chance at the job. And it turned out that the years of experience, in life especially, made me better prepared the third time around.

Many rules of successful communication seem obvious until you realize how frequently they're ignored in favor of expediency and avoiding awkwardness. To successfully navigate a difficult conversation, the first step is to accept mutual discomfort as inevitable. If you have to be the bearer of bad news, you carry much of this weight at the outset: you're the one who can prepare for the conversation, and if you approach it sensitively, you can help the person you're speaking with manage and understand their own response. Still, you might worry that you'll somehow make the upsetting conversation worse by misspeaking at a vulnerable moment, or you might fear a negative reaction—anger, tears, or the classic blaming the messenger.

My experience losing out on the press secretary job in 2014 taught me to take my responsibilities as a manager seriously. When I conduct a job search and land on a candidate, I ensure there are plans in place to contact other finalists and let them know we're going in another direction, before the new hire is announced. Some human resources departments don't allow hiring managers to take this step, and that's too bad—even when we just want to get them over with, all difficult conversations are an opportunity to demonstrate sensitivity and care.

The method of delivering bad news is also vital to developing clear and effective communication patterns. Getting on the phone is tougher (sometimes *much* tougher) for the caller than just sending an email; even easier than sending an email is avoiding the issue altogether and letting time or fate deliver the news. While it's also sometimes true that it can be easier for the recipient to get an email instead of having to manage their emotional reaction in person, hiring managers' tendency to assume that no one wants to receive that call is often simply an excuse to avoid doing what's uncomfortable. If you can't make a phone call, email may be your only option, but at least make sure the rejected candidate gets word as soon as someone else has accepted the job.

Of course, some professional experiences are much worse than not getting a job you wanted. Throughout my early career, I never had to fire anyone. One of the risks of hiring good people, particularly the kind of people with relentless curiosity whom I gravitate toward, is that they tend to move on. Typically, they're the ones who eventually give me bad news, not vice versa. That changed when I was overseeing the communications team at the Carnegie Endowment for International Peace in 2017. We were about to launch a massive $100 million fundraising campaign, and communications would be playing a major role in that effort. I needed to make a few personnel changes to the team in order to bring in different skill sets.

In the days leading up to these conversations, I constantly felt like I was going to throw up. Though this may surprise some people on the right wing, I am not a fan of personal confrontation, and did not want to have to fire anyone. In my panic, I asked a few trusted former colleagues for advice. One of them was Jeff Zients, who became President Biden's chief of staff in 2023 and at the time was working in the private sector. He told me that I needed to be direct in delivering the news and while it was important to be kind, I could not let the exchange devolve into a discussion of why this was happening, or whether there was any way to reverse the decision. I should avoid the temptation to overexplain, which would require a number of twists and turns that might veer into dishonesty. In almost no case does hard news become easier to hear when it's wrapped in a soliloquy. People can tell when you're avoiding the uncomfortable truth of the situation.

I prepared some language to make sure I didn't go off course. I wanted to be empathetic and not too harsh; firm but fair. So, when I initiated these meetings, I said something like "I'm grateful for your time at the Carnegie Endowment, and you've made important contributions during your time here. But we've decided to go in a different direction with your position, and your final day here will be in three weeks."

I conveyed gratitude but kept it to the point. In one case, a younger employee wanted to know why he was being let go; I briefly said that it was time for him to grow in a different place. Another longtime employee expressed shock at the decision, but I simply stuck with my points that I was grateful for her years there and that we just needed a different skill set for the next stage. Neither was a particularly easy conversation. I knew these responses would be dissatisfying to someone dealing with the surprise and fear that losing a job causes. But I also knew I had to balance the demands of my own role with my responsibility to treat them with respect.

* * *

If the only tough conversations we had to have were about our jobs, life would be pretty easy. But no matter how much you love your job— even if you love it too much—it's just a job. The most difficult conversations usually involve news that takes place outside the office. Illness, death, and tragedy are facts of life, and while hearing bad news can be very, very hard, hearing nothing can be devastating.

When I was eight years old, my grandmother on my dad's side passed away. This is always a difficult moment in a family, and she was only sixty-six years old. Unfortunately, there's not more lead-up to this story, because no one was prepared for her death. Just before Thanksgiving that year, my grandparents told the family that Grandma was a little under the weather and she wouldn't make it to the big turkey dinner. She died a few days later. She had had lung cancer, a diagnosis only my grandfather knew about until she died from it.

My dad would say his parents were emotionally unavailable. He grew up in a military family, and they were products of that culture in the 1940s, '50s, and '60s; they moved around all the time, and it was not an atmosphere of openness, or one in which it was acceptable to talk about your emotions. What's more, my grandmother's mother died when my grandmother was a toddler—for her generation, it might have been easier to accept the death of a parent as a fact of life. My grandmother was also a chain smoker, and probably an alcoholic, though she never would have referred to herself as that. My grandfather also struggled with alcohol. Again, this was not a generation that talked a lot about the challenges they were facing. But the context makes it easier to understand their choices now.

I was a kid at the time—I didn't really understand what was going on. My parents told us that our grandmother had died, but it was only when I was older that the impact of this event dawned on me.

Over decades, I watched how this choice to avoid the difficult conversation affected my father's relationship with his dad—my grandfather—as well as my uncle's relationship with him. By the time my grandfather died, the rift wasn't fully repaired. I can now see that my dad was around my age when his mother died, and I can only imagine what it might be like to go through something so disorienting and destabilizing without the benefit of any warning. It would make you forever suspicious of your own memories, learning that such a major secret was kept from you. And denying you the chance to say goodbye to your mother is hard to forgive. Illness and difficult news often prompt people to avoid communication. My grandparents may have kept quiet because they didn't want to upset the family, which can be seen as a loving gesture, in its own way. Or my grandparents may have felt that by controlling what the rest of the family knew, they were asserting control in a situation that was, devastatingly, beyond their ability to do anything about. Or maybe they were in denial. It's not the obligation of someone who is suffering to spread that news, even if those who would have liked to have known will be upset when they learn what happened. But once you do know something, a conversation starts, whether you realize it, or want it to, or not. You are always communicating, even when you say nothing. When you withhold important, life-changing information from those you love, or even when you avoid acknowledging a tough situation out of fear, you are still saying something.

Regardless of how you intend to approach a difficult conversation, fear is the mother of procrastination. Procrastination is almost always bad—I actually can't think of a situation in which it's beneficial—but it's especially a problem when it comes to having these kinds of necessary talks. As Glennon Doyle puts it in her book *Untamed* and talks about on her podcast, *We Can Do Hard Things*, sometimes you need to "eat the frog." This phrase allegedly comes from Mark Twain, who is quoted as having said, "Eat a live frog first thing in the morning and nothing worse will happen to you the rest of the day." In recent years, this has been transformed into productivity advice: do the task that you're dreading the most first, and everything that follows will feel easy. I prefer the quickest frog-eating method possible. The longer you wait, the more consequences—both emotional and logistical—you can expect. Putting it off will only make you keep thinking about how much you don't want to eat a slimy amphibian—and that may produce an outcome worse than you originally feared.

Sometimes just showing up is the only thing anyone can do for people who are suffering or grieving. In a highly charged emotional situation, you might feel pressure to come up with the perfect message to offer to someone in pain, but there's no such thing. When a friend of mine was diagnosed with breast cancer in her twenties it was shocking. No one knew what to say or how to comfort her, and we were all afraid. The best course of action, which I learned from her at the time, was just to say *something*, almost anything. It didn't have to be perfect—and it couldn't have been. The deeply spiritual may take comfort in the reassurance that what they're going through is all part of a divine plan. Others may be offended by the idea that there is any justifiable reason for what's happened. For some, statistics can be a source of comfort; for others, facts and figures downplay the emotional significance of the problem. As always, knowing whom you're talking to, and understanding the context of the situation, is important. But the biggest hurt can come not from what is said, but what isn't. In my friend's case, people she had known for years didn't check in. Friends she expected to visit didn't follow through. She felt that she'd been forgotten.

Nobody wants to be forgotten, looked down on, or ignored. That's why a president showing up after a tragedy can be so meaningful to those who have suffered. There isn't anyone in the world who has a busier, more complicated, and more important job—but a good president knows this is an important use of his time. It isn't ever going to be enough, but hopefully, for a little while, it can be a solace.

In May of 2021, President Biden announced his plans to withdraw all troops from Afghanistan. It was a huge undertaking, involving major risks. More than 3,000 Americans had already died in the conflict, and during the chaotic and dangerous evacuations more lives were lost when an Islamic State suicide bomber attacked the Kabul airport. Approximately 170 Afghan civilians died, as well as 13 members of the American military.

Two days after those American service members were killed at Abbey Gate in Afghanistan, their bodies arrived at Dover Air Force Base, where the president and First Lady joined the grieving families. Of all the president's duties, this is high on the list of most heartbreaking. For President Biden in particular, it stirred feelings of his own despair about the death of his son Joseph Biden III, aka Beau, from cancer in 2015. Beau Biden had served in Iraq for almost a year, with stints at Camp Victory in Baghdad and the Balad Air Force base. While there is no conclusive data on what caused Beau's glioblastoma, an aggressive type of brain cancer that he battled for several years, both these bases used "burn pits" that sent large volumes of toxic particulate matter into the air. The World Health Organization's cancer research arm has classified some of the chemical substances found in burn pit emissions as "known to be carcinogenic to humans."

Decades before he lost Beau, the president's first wife and daughter had died in a car accident; the president often refers to these unique and disparate, but nevertheless unbearable, experiences of grief and loss as a way to connect with others. That day in Dover, the president and First Lady spent hours speaking with and consoling the family members who lost loved ones in the terrorist attack in Kabul. Sadly, that day's visit quickly became controversial because of a combination of misinformation and miscommunication. The misinformation came in the form of a single photo of the president looking at his watch during the ceremony. People who are quick to criticize the president seized on this image. They splashed it all over social media, making him appear insensitive, concerned only about how much time had passed. A glance became a story. There was such an uproar that the *Washington Post* reviewed video of the event and concluded: "Footage leading up to the moment . . . shows Biden with his hand over his heart . . . as vans carry the service members' remains off the tarmac. After the vans left, Biden closed his eyes briefly before dropping his arm and glancing down at his watch." In other words, the president only looked at his watch after the ceremony had ended. Moments later, he and the First Lady headed toward their car. But by the time this correction was issued, the image was already circulating, and the damage had been done.

That would have been distressing enough, but then some family members of the soldiers started speaking out with complaints. They said that the president had talked too much about his son Beau and hadn't focused enough on their own tragedies. The *New York Times* pounced on this emotionally charged dynamic and started working on a large Sunday story about how the death of Beau had affected the president, with the visit to Dover and the family's complaints as the central story line.

The president was not new to unflattering media stories; there had been plenty of negative press about his campaign and his son Hunter's struggle with addiction. But Beau was rarely, if ever, the focus of a negative story, and I was new to telling the president that a tough story was coming. It was one thing to tell the president that the media was planning to criticize his COVID response, and quite another to say that the media was planning to criticize the way he speaks about his son, who passed away tragically young. I realized in this moment that *this* was what I had been preparing for in the time since I first sat down with President Biden and Dr. Biden to discuss the role. I also realized I could not really comprehend the pain he had suffered, and knew I needed to keep that in mind when figuring out how to break this news to him.

I thought back to when he and I had first discussed my joining his administration. That day, I had waited at a large round conference table in a room with big windows for the future president and First Lady to make their way out of the event where he had announced his national security team. Because of my work for President Obama, this wasn't my first time meeting the Bidens. The president-elect and I had crossed paths at many meetings, but we didn't really know each other personally. Still, he greeted me warmly and then spoke about the campaign, foreign policy, and the impact of the Trump presidency. He asked me a few questions about how I viewed politics in the country, and then Dr. Biden asked if I had any questions for them. I really wanted the job, and knew I was ready for it. So, I was prepared with the right question—and speaking from her unfathomable experience, she was prepared with the right answer.

"How can I work best with you?" I asked.

"We have been through a lot," Dr. Biden replied. "And we ask that you always be honest with us. Always tell us what is coming."

Now it was on me to fulfill that request. As soon as I heard about the *New York Times* story, I wrote down some notes at my desk and called the president from my office in the West Wing. It was a Saturday morning—not the time you want to make or receive this kind of call.

"Sir, I wanted you to know that there is a *New York Times* story coming out tomorrow that will talk about how you referenced Beau's death repeatedly while meeting with the families of the soldiers who were killed in Afghanistan last week," I began. "It will quote a number of family members making critical comments about how much you talked about your son during these interactions."

After laying out the problem, I turned to the response. I walked the president through the steps we had already taken to explain how his grief had affected him, and I gave him a direct summary of how I thought the story would land. (Not well, but we would handle it.)

I paused for the president to respond. The silence that followed was a bit too long. I worried for a moment that our connection had been lost.

"Sir, are you still there?" I asked.

He answered in a softer voice than usual.

"I thought I was helping them. Hearing about how other people went through loss always helped me," he said. There was another pause. "Thanks for telling me. Anything else?"

"No, sir, that was all I wanted to update you on. I am sorry this story is happening."

I had been direct, which is what he and Dr. Biden had requested. It was the best I could do in such a tense, emotionally fraught situation. Still, it was deeply unfortunate that we had to discuss how a news story would be received by millions of people when its subject was something so personal, and still so painful, to the president. But that was part of the job.

I knew there would be more fallout once the article was printed and journalists called for comments or brought it up in the next press briefing. When that happened, I made it clear that it was "certainly the right of any individual who met with the president yesterday to speak publicly about their experience." Then I offered my clarification of the president's intention in bringing up Beau. "While his son did not lose his life directly in combat as they did—or directly at the hands of a terrorist, as these families did that they're mourning—he knows firsthand that there's nothing you can say, nothing you can convey, to ease the pain and to ease what all these families are going through." I wanted to express that words can't heal this kind of loss, but they can offer support, solace, or simple acknowledgment, and that understanding was what the Bidens were trying to convey to these families.

Finally, I restated an absolute truth: the president's "message to all of the family members who were there, those who were not even in attendance, is that he is grateful to their sons and daughters, the sacrifice they made to the country." I established that I would not discuss President Biden's experience, or his private conversations, further, but I did add a final point from my own perspective. "I will tell you, from spending a lot of time with him over the past couple of days, that he was deeply impacted by these family members who he met just two days ago," I said. "That he talks about them frequently in meetings and the incredible service and sacrifice of their sons and daughters. That is not going to change their suffering, but I wanted to convey that still."

Difficult conversations don't follow a uniform pattern. Those related to your professional life are almost always best if short, honest, and timely. If your objective is to just say no or "I'm sorry, this isn't working out," the shorter and more direct, the better. But if you want to provide support, it's a little different. When it comes to more personal issues, the best approach can vary wildly, and depends on the context. How long have you known each other? What do you know about each other? No matter what's going on, avoidance doesn't transform bad news into good, or make inherently uncomfortable conversations more fluid. Avoidance only makes things temporarily easier for the person who is responsible for speaking up. Presence matters. You don't need to offer long speeches. Sometimes, when the conversation is difficult, just being there, silent, and with a clock nowhere to be seen, can be the pinnacle of successful communication.

* * *

As a parent, I'm grateful I haven't yet had to have any truly difficult conversations with my children. I know they will come sooner or later. But the closest I've come to having to explain something tragic to them still showed me the power of direct communication. It happened a couple of summers ago, when Greg and I had to tell them our dog died.

We'd gone to visit my husband's parents in Ohio and to see some friends in Kentucky, and a friend's daughter was watching our eight-year-old mini schnauzer, Greta, at her house. When we returned, our nephew had a birthday party, so I took the kids there while my husband went to pick up the dog.

Not long into the party, I got a call from Greg: Greta couldn't breathe. Things quickly became hectic. I tried not to let my emotions show as the kids enjoyed the party; Greg was rushing Greta to the vet. There was nothing I could do over the phone so I let Greg handle it. Soon after, he called back: Greta didn't make it.

The minute I heard, I worried about how we would tell the kids. I didn't want to traumatize them, and I certainly wasn't going to break up the party, but I knew I'd have to do it as soon as we got home and they realized Greta wasn't there. Like me, my mother is a professional talker, but as a practicing therapist she is slightly more serene. I pulled her aside at the party to let her know our dog died. What was I going to say to the kids?

My mom's advice was to be straightforward, direct, and light on gruesome details. I needed to create a forum for the kids to share their feelings, rather than unload my own stress and sadness. I didn't want to push them to respond but instead allow them to react in their own way. I also did not need to tell them the entire chaotic story of Greta's untimely death. (Which I will also spare you here.)

"Greta has passed away," I said to the kids as soon as we got back to our house and they were settled at the kitchen counter. "She's going to be in heaven."

Did they know what that meant? Did I even know what I meant? I made sure to acknowledge that they might not know what to do with this information, and to make them feel safe to express themselves. "It's OK to feel any way you want to feel," I added, "and you can ask any questions about it."

They didn't say much then about Greta, or for a couple of days, which was hard for me. What were they thinking? Were they OK? Finally, my son, who was four years old at the time, asked a question: "Does this mean we'll never meet Nana's mommy?" He had connected the two losses—those of his great-grandmother and his dog—and somehow realized that death is final.

My daughter, who is named after this grandma, holds her cards close to her chest. We didn't hear much from her about Greta until a couple of months later, around Christmastime. As per tradition, we hung a stocking for Greta. One day, our daughter took out a piece of paper, wrote my mom's dog's name on it, and placed it over Greta's name.

Vivi, too, had come to a realization about death, and she had processed it in her own way, on her own timeline, before I got to see how her feelings manifested. A difficult conversation can be an opportunity to get to know people in a different way—even your children. It can also become an opportunity to open up an aperture in a relationship—to see more of the possibilities than you had before.

This was most obvious in my family when, after years of being in a relationship with a man, my sister Kristen told us she was attracted to women. A few years later, she began seeing a person who at the time identified as a woman. As their relationship progressed, her partner, Andie, came out as trans. By this time we knew Andie as an amazing cook, a lover of animals and nature, and most of all a supportive partner to our sister. We also knew, being a family of big talkers, we would have a lot of conversations about how to be supportive and we wouldn't always get it right.

We all wanted to make sure we were speaking with Andie in a respectful way, and we wanted to make talking with us about his transition easier, if he wanted to speak to us about it at all. At first, though, we didn't know what to say. How do you show support without being pushy, or asking too many questions? With Andie, we didn't want him to feel obligated to educate us, but we also didn't want him to feel like we didn't care. We also worried that our kids might misgender Andie accidentally, given that they'd gotten to know him under different pronouns.

So we were a bit awkward at first, and quiet, which, as we've learned, is not the best communication strategy. We didn't want him to be uncomfortable. And as a result, he felt that we were uncomfortable. All tough spots seem to come from this same basic principle: one person making assumptions about the other person's feelings, and treading too lightly, allowing the misunderstanding to grow.

We quickly realized that children are much more adaptable than adults, who have had outdated ways of thinking about gender ingrained in our stubborn brains.

We focused on figuring out the best tone for questions that made everyone feel safe. There is a clear difference between curiosity that comes from a prurient and judgmental place and curiosity that comes from an attempt to learn more about someone you love. Something open-ended like "So you're taking hormones—what does that mean? What do they do?" is much easier to respond to than something like "Do hormones make you grow facial hair?" When the questions are sensitive and respectful, more of them are almost always better than fewer.

Our family has good intentions, but we are also completely imperfect. I am certain it's been frustrating for Kristen and Andie at times.

And I have to say: it's mostly Andie's and Kristen's openness to discussion that has allowed us to grow as a family and learn to communicate in a truly open way. Sometimes we want things to be black-and-white, but it is the gray areas that make for the best conversations. There is often no right thing to say. Sometimes the talks backfire; sometimes they fizzle out. But in rare instances, they help everyone involved deepen their relationships.

5

What the Heck Is a "Non-Filer"?

*On the importance of building and conveying trust,
credibility, and expertise as a communicator*

Working for John Kerry, I learned a lot about optimism and the importance
of preserving your credibility. Here we are seated on a train to Paris after
the government plane broke down during a whirlwind 2014 diplomatic
trip.

In 2006, psychologist Daniel M. Oppenheimer, then at Princeton
University, wrote a landmark paper called "Consequences of Erudite
Vernacular Utilized Irrespective of Necessity." Talk about a difficult conver-
sation. You probably skipped over a few of those words. Try again. I'll wait.

Easier to process is the paper's subtitle: "Problems with Using Long
Words Needlessly." Oppenheimer conducted a series of experiments

that identified the gap between academic and everyday language and tested assumptions about whether a complex vocabulary makes a person seem more intelligent. His conclusion was something everyone who hopes to be a good communicator should keep front and center: "write as simply and plainly as possible and it's more likely you'll be thought of as intelligent."

This is not just advice that applies to people in positions of authority; it can be expanded to apply to pretty much any conversation. There are very few situations in which you'd *want* to confuse your audience or, worse, prompt them to tune you out or resent you for confusing them or talking down to them. But there are a few things you can do to set yourself up to be listened to—even by people who'd prefer to ignore what you have to say.

In early February 2021, President Biden was practicing a speech he was about to deliver to the country on the American Rescue Plan. During a break between run-throughs, he sat down with me at a table in the State Dining Room and asked me what questions reporters had about the proposal. This legislation was major; it was designed to put the economy back on better footing and hopefully get the impacts of COVID under control, and part of it included delivering checks to people who needed help after the devastating effects of the pandemic. Because receiving a check from the government is a rare occurrence that might have sounded too good to be true, it was important that I communicate the immediate benefits of the bill to the American people as straightforwardly as possible: more than 85 percent of households would receive a check. The president asked me how I intended to explain that the federal payments would extend to people who didn't make enough income to file taxes. This was a small percentage of the public, but a major concern of his. I'd prepared an answer.

"Well, I start by saying, 'For anyone who is a non-filer—'"

He stopped me before I finished the sentence.

"What the heck is a non-filer?" he asked, loudly. "No one speaks like that."

My cheeks flushed. I'm used to critical feedback, but it never feels great in the moment, especially when it's coming from the president of the United States just a month into a new job. But as soon as he repeated the term "non-filer," I knew he was right. While "non-filer" was succinct (less is more!) and technically correct, it was internal jargon. When I said it out loud, I sounded like I was in a procedural drama about accountants gone rogue. Immediately, I changed the language.

"Anyone who is a non-filer" became "anyone who may not make enough money to file taxes or isn't sure whether or not they are qualified." While this was a lot longer than "anyone who is a non-filer," in this case, saying more was less confusing. Just as the bill described in chapter 1, the Bipartisan Infrastructure Framework, became the plan to "rebuild roads, railways and bridges and make sure kids have clean drinking water," the COVID outreach plan became "reaching people in their communities to make it easier to find vaccines and ask questions about vaccines." In all that "longhand shorthand" was language that told a story and helped frame the discussion.

You might wonder why I ever said something like "non-filer" in the first place. It certainly wasn't the way I would have described such a person when speaking with anyone in my family, or anyone I knew who hadn't worked in the federal government. (And even then, its utility was limited—I probably would have said "a person who doesn't have to file taxes.") But almost all of us, in almost every situation, can be tempted to show off how smart we are. Maybe we think that signaling our expertise will be a shortcut to winning over our audience, or winning an argument, or simply impressing whomever we're talking to. The word "non-filer" sounds official and insider-y—that's maybe why I reached for it in the moment. That's also why it might have alienated my audience.

As I got comfortable in the press secretary job, I began to think about whether what I was saying would pass what I thought of as the mother-in-law test. My husband's mom, Mary Ann, is a retired teacher in Cincinnati, Ohio. She is smart, loves to read, and pays attention to the news; you can have an engaging conversation with her about pretty much any contemporary political issue. But, like most people, she doesn't speak the language of Washington, DC—from inside-baseball references like "the Squad" (the group of several young progressives elected to the House of Representatives in 2018 and 2020) to intricate legislative processes like "budget reconciliation" (it's actually too complicated to explain in this parenthetical). And why should she? When I'm explaining an issue or a debate in Washington to anyone outside the Beltway (the highway that encircles DC and also a term used to refer to federal government insiders), I often consider if Mary Ann would know what I'm talking about before I use a particular word or phrase. There are some—but not many—acronyms that have become so well known, and omnipresent in the media, that it would be silly not to use them. "NASA" is indisputably preferable to "the National Aeronautics and Space Administration." But there were several times at the State Department when public talking points were approved with such inspiring language as "Consistent with UNSCR 5043 . . . ," which was totally useless for anyone listening who didn't work at the UN, cover the UN, or—well, that was it.[*] There was also a large crew of people who tried to nickname the previously mentioned Bipartisan Infrastructure Framework "BIF." If you would like your audience to start making fun of a big, serious, and important piece of legislation, start calling it BIF.

We all have a "mother-in-law" who can serve as our hypothetical

---

[*] For those with further curiosity about UNSCR 5043 and the language used in United Nations Security Council resolutions, I suggest the 1,330-page *Repertoire of the Practice of the Security Council.* It's online.

critic—we just have to be willing to listen to them. As is always the case with good communication, your ego can be the biggest impediment to understanding. Ironically, it's often the smartest, most educated people who struggle to learn this lesson. How many times have you been at a doctor's appointment, waiting a little impatiently for the consultation, only to have the clinician present you with a litany of medical terms that you *kind of* understand, but actually maybe not? And then when he asks if you have any questions, you feel you don't want to get clarification because you'll sound like an idiot, and he seems rushed, and you're not sure you are smart enough to understand any of it anyway?

"Every patient wants their doctor to be academically prepared—to know the medicine that they need to know," says Darrell Kirch, president and CEO of the Association of American Medical Colleges. "But equally important, they want their doctors to have personal attributes that contribute to their professionalism—what a patient might call their 'bedside manner.'" When you're in that consultation room and thinking your doctor might as well be speaking Greek, the information they're providing isn't wrong—in fact, for the experts who wield the scalpels and write the prescriptions, it's more "right" than a less precise summary. But in most cases, overly formal academic language leaves the patient annoyed, confused, and maybe even scared. According to a study in the *American Journal of Emergency Medicine*, the percentage of hospital patients who didn't know that "hemorrhage" meant "bleeding" was 79 percent. The same was true when it came to words like "fractured" for "broken" (78 percent), and "myocardial infarction" for "heart attack" (74 percent)—because the doctors and nurses never effectively explained to their patients what was happening to them.

Of course, there are a lot of great doctors out there, and a good number of them are fantastic at communicating what's going on. But this extreme example illustrates a crucial principle of communication: only among fellow experts does it improve clarity to express your expertise through industry-specific language. Both as press secretary and in my current job at MSNBC, I'm often tasked with translating complicated issues for broad audiences, and over time I've realized I can set the tone for a discussion with an expert by asking clearly phrased, direct questions in language that most people will understand. If I sense my interviewee is veering off track, I can steer them back to stable ground by keeping my own language simple, and by rephrasing their statements in simpler language to guide both them and the viewer to mutual understanding. Unloading extremely detailed information on the public about recent clashes on the Kyrgyzstan-Tajikistan border, for example, is a lot like a doctor burying you in an avalanche of medical terms that only a specialist in the field would understand. People will tune you out.

It makes sense that a historian of Central Asia would want to talk for hours about the border between Kyrgyzstan and Tajikistan: they've studied the territory for years, they speak the relevant languages, they have personal relationships with people from both countries, and they've tasted *shorpo shorpo* (a famous—to them—Kyrgyz soup). But the majority of the American public isn't especially interested in hearing hours' worth of information about Kyrgyzstan and Tajikistan. It may be compelling once you learn more, but the fact is that if you dumped a bunch of unfiltered information about this region on the general population, they'd end up caring *less*, not more, about what was going on there than when you started—which is the definition of unsuccessful communication. That sudden disinterest doesn't arise just because you've bored them, but because people are turned off by words and concepts they don't recognize or understand—particularly if the things they don't recognize aren't just fancy vocabulary words, but terms that are basically inaccessible without graduate-level study in that very specific topic. When the speaker has some sort of formal authority, the overwhelmed audience doesn't just get lost while listening; they may feel affronted. Even if the point is to educate, the audience interprets all the new details and terminology as a means to exclude them from the conversation, signaling that the issue at hand is above their pay grade. It's not about being dumb or lazy—it's that not everyone can or should be a doctor or a historian of Central Asia. Most of us have our own variety of expertise that would transform us into an incomprehensible talking head if we were allowed to expound on it for several minutes.

To quote President Obama's unofficial catchphrase, "let me be clear": we need experts. This is not an argument against expertise. You might not like your doctor's bedside manner, but the most important thing is that he went to medical school and knows more than you do about how the body works and what to do when it doesn't. You need a great physician. You want a great communicator. In a perfect world, your doctor would be both, but it's not a perfect world.

If an audience doesn't have any interest in learning something they didn't know, or even having their views challenged, you're going to come up against the limits of what you can discuss with them—no matter how clear and simple your language. But one of the metrics of successful communication is sparking interest. To engage, you sometimes need to meet people where they are, in terms of their knowledge and potential interest in a given topic. You also need to keep an open mind—people can surprise you with what they know, what they're curious about, and how much complex information they can consume. Every expert I worked with in the White House and State Department once knew nothing about their area of expertise. And thanks to all the news coverage she consumed, my mother-in-law quickly knew enough about Russia's invasion of Ukraine to comprehensively talk about weapons systems. But sparking that interest and curiosity often requires engaging in a direct and accessible way, instead of starting a discussion at the PhD level.

*   *   *

A deluge of terminology doesn't only elicit confusion; it can also draw skepticism, and make your audience think you're trying to hide a *lack* of expertise—or, at least, to disguise an inability to come up with a solution. A barrage of technical language may also be an insulting way to deflect responsibility for things gone wrong. As Daniel Pink, a former speechwriter for Vice President Al Gore and assistant to Robert Reich when he was labor secretary, has noted, "it takes more cognitive effort for a company to come up with this ridiculous, 'We're sorry for any inconvenience this might have caused you,' rather than saying, 'Oh my God, we're so sorry, we messed up.'" Not only is the first version leaden, but it also shifts the statement from directly admitting a mistake to more of a "things happen . . ." shrug. We've all been on the line when a customer service representative says, "We're sorry for any inconvenience." What you hear is that they aren't sorry at all. Jargon and bureaucratese have a way of doing that.

If you use this kind of language when you're trying to communicate *good* news, it's even worse. When I worked in the Obama administration and we were trying to sell the Affordable Care Act, or ACA, to the American public back in 2009, we repeatedly told people that the bill would "bend the cost curve." The phrase is a reference to a curve on a graph, and in the context of the ACA, it meant the policy would save Americans money on healthcare. Didn't everyone want to save money on healthcare? To sell this message, we had charts and curvy graphs and more data than you can imagine. Government officials love data and graphs.

The phrase "bend the cost curve" is just like "non-filer": it's jargon that is more likely to prompt people to tune out rather than engage. Meanwhile, Sarah Palin was lying that the bill proposed "death panels" that would allow bureaucrats to determine when the elderly or people with medical conditions were worthy of medical care—a claim that, while false, spoke to emotional concerns. Palin's line, and other conservative fear tactics, helped Republicans triumph in the next three electoral waves in part because of these lies about the intent and potential impact of the ACA. Opponents of Bill Clinton's failed effort to reform the health system in the 1990s had successfully exploited the comprehensiveness of his bill to their advantage, presenting it as evidence of despotic federal overreach. (The most successful TV ads against the bill featured actors mentioning not only aspects of the plan they were "concerned" about but also which page in the bill they were from, reinforcing the idea that such a long document was bound to be bloated and incoherent.)

After the ACA passed and was signed into law in 2010, despite his own history of passing a similarly expansive healthcare bill as governor of Massachusetts, Mitt Romney hammered away at the program's cost when he was running against Obama in 2012. Romney's argument was that if we kept the ACA, Americans would be stuck with health insurance bills way higher than what they were already paying, and without the ability to choose their own doctors. It tapped into the emotional fears that skeptics had about the legislation, making it an effective criticism.

President Obama needed to get back to the human-centered stories that propelled him to the White House in his first term—and he did. Gradually. The charts went into a storage closet, and emotional storytelling took center stage. Now the focus shifted to people whose lives had literally been saved by the ACA, including cancer survivors who could not be kicked off their insurance under the bill's provisions. Since nearly every family had a member with a preexisting condition, this became a big selling point. We talked about how mothers were receiving a greater level of prenatal care, how parents could now keep their children on the family healthcare plan until the age of twenty-six, and how the law prohibited insurance companies from charging sick people more than people who were healthy. It was much more effective than talking about the bill's historic nature and "cost curve bending impact."

I know firsthand how easy it is to fall back on bad communication habits, especially when you're nervous or under pressure. One Sunday in February 2021, just over a month into my stint as White House press secretary, I was slated to do a few Sunday morning TV shows, including Fox News. The Biden administration had just reengaged with the leaders of Saudi Arabia, which was challenging to communicate about on many levels. First and foremost, there was the fact that the crown prince had been accused of ordering the torture and murder of *Washington Post* reporter Jamal Khashoggi in Istanbul. During the election, candidate Biden had gone on the record saying that the country's rulers should be "pariahs." Given this strong condemnation, it was entirely valid for journalists to ask me the question: Why was the United States having talks with these leaders?

Predictably, that's what I was asked during every interview that day. I responded by pointing out that the administration believed Khashoggi's murder was a horrific crime and we had taken action against Saudi Arabia, including applying sanctions. I also talked about the lack of precedent for sanctioning a head of state. Then, on Fox, I concluded by insisting to host Chris Wallace that we'd taken "very specific steps to make sure we're sending a clear message to the world."

Wallace pounced.

"But it isn't a clear message," he said, accurately.

He continued to press me on the issue, and I just started spewing everything I knew about US–Saudi Arabia relations. I figured that the more expertise I displayed, the more credibility I'd have when saying there was a clear message, even if there really wasn't one. In retrospect, what I should have done was acknowledge the difficulty of the choices that you make as commander in chief and emphasize that, for the president, that meant engaging with the leaders of Saudi Arabia because it was in our national security interests, even as we had major concerns about their human rights record. And I should have delivered that message at about half the speed.

It was early in my new job, and I was clearly nervous, but I walked away hoping I'd pulled it off—if I didn't exactly respond to Wallace's comment, well, isn't that a fairly common occurrence in tough interviews? Those hopes were dashed as soon as I checked my phone. During the interview, my husband, sister, and brother-in-law had been texting about plans for later that afternoon, and they included some thoughts on my performance. "That was not her best," my normally very supportive husband commented. "She was talking really fast."

Yeah, they forgot I was on the chain, too. (Another rule of successful communication that I've broken a few times: always check the cc: list.)

Greg was right. There's an old saying: "When you're on thin ice, skate fast." But when it comes to successful communication, you make the ice thinner by skating quickly. When you're communicating about a difficult subject under time pressure, the only thing speaking quickly accomplishes is to muddle your message and make it difficult to understand. In rare cases—like when you're being asked questions that are impossible to answer without making yourself or your employer look bad—distracting your audience by babbling for several minutes *may* be what you want to do, but you will lose credibility in the process. Most of the time, you should stay calm, crisp, and thoughtful without trying to cram in as many points as possible. Anyone who has given a presentation of any sort—fifth-grade book report, wedding toast, sales pitch—has heard the classic advice: *speak slowly*. Even slower than you think. A couple of points delivered clearly and confidently are worth much more than twenty-seven ideas expressed in a rush.

* * *

A common mistake people make is thinking they need to have an answer to every question. But there are some questions that simply have no answer. There were times when I was the press secretary where the best response I could offer was along the lines of "This is a difficult issue, and there are difficult choices. None of them are great." Acknowledging that complexity can deflate the balloon a bit. The journalists I was speaking to knew that issues like our relations with Saudi Arabia were not straightforward. (If they were, they would have been resolved years ago and reporters would have nothing to produce stories about.) While it may sound counterintuitive, acknowledging that something is complicated can do more to connect you with the person asking the question. If you say an obviously complicated issue is easy, your audience may think you're uninformed, or trying to manipulate them into believing your view.

Trying to communicate in a private setting isn't the same as doing so in a White House press conference, but similar dynamics exist with audiences of any size. If you give a wrong answer, and then stand by it, the only thing you're communicating is that you're untrustworthy. Taking responsibility when you don't know the answer is part of what gives you credibility. Doing it clearly and honestly is what makes you a good communicator. And adeptly taking responsibility when you've given the wrong answer is what makes you a very good communicator.

When I was working for John Kerry at the State Department in early July 2013, the first democratically elected president of Egypt, Mohamed Morsi, was deposed in a military coup. Shortly after, a CBS journalist tweeted a photo of Kerry's yacht in Nantucket, reporting that my boss had been spotted onboard as the unrest began in Egypt— terrible optics for an American secretary of state.

It was the night before July Fourth, and I was out with friends at fireworks trying to enjoy a rare break from work. I attempted to deal with this report as quickly as possible after a brief and noisy phone call with one of Kerry's traveling aides; I quickly issued a statement denying the report: "Since his plane touched down in Washington at 4:00 AM, Secretary Kerry was working all day and on the phone dealing with the crisis in Egypt." I also firmly denied the accuracy of the story to a number of respected reporters.

I believed this was true at the time, but as it turned out, I had spoken too soon. CBS was right: my boss *had* been on his yacht on the day in question. I hadn't intended to deceive—my mistake had been the result of both a bad phone connection and then not doing due diligence with one of my bosses about the details, though I know this is exactly the sort of "likely story" nobody trusts.

After getting the full story from Kerry—which is what I should have done in the first place—I called CBS to confess that I had made a mistake, and to say he had been on his boat that day. Then I called every single reporter I had spoken to about the story and fell on my sword for unintentionally providing inaccurate information. I also shared the additional detail that on that day he had also taken a short break to walk around the seaside town to get some fresh air but otherwise had been on the phone discussing the situation in Egypt more or less nonstop.

Again, veteran reporters have context. Once they got the full story, they understood that I hadn't been attempting a nefarious plot to trick them: I genuinely misunderstood my colleague on a phone call in the middle of loud fireworks (literally there were fireworks in the background; it was July 3) and hadn't known my boss was on his yacht.

I did have other options for dealing with this mistake, and some of them would have saved me a headache in the short term. I could have remained silent and hoped the story went away, as most news stories do, particularly those that emerge during a high-stakes coup d'état. Or I could have pointed fingers, claiming the allegations were a conspiracy designed to harm my boss, who had famously been the victim of a smear campaign accusing him of lying about his military career when he ran for president in 2004. But instead, I asked myself a question—*the* question: *What do you want your reputation to be?* I knew exactly what I had to do. I got some flak from the press, and I felt like a fool for embarrassing my boss, but the next day, I was back to full steam ahead.

Sometimes it's the little things that catch up to you. If you think it's OK not to own up to your mistakes when they're minor—if you assume you can pave over those potholes in your credibility before you have to handle a more serious situation—you're wrong. Why would you be trusted with major issues if you have a bad track record with the easy stuff? While the Nantucket yacht scandal wasn't ever going to be subject to the Woodward-Bernstein treatment, my quick apology and clarification made me more trustworthy. That I was willing to take the time to personally contact all the people I thought would feel misled made my good intentions more evident and appreciated.

If you want to be a truly successful communicator, you have to be cred-ible. In fact, credibility is one of the most important factors in helping an audience determine whether you're right about something. It's even more essential when you're making the case that your audience should pay attention to you even when what you're saying doesn't match what they want to hear. Each time you lose another layer of your credibility, it's harder and harder to regain trust.

As we've seen, developing credibility can often mean making a choice between your status in the short term and your reputation in the long term. What happens when the event determining your cred-ibility isn't a relatively minor news item attached to a major story, but the story itself?

On the Saturday after Trump's inauguration, then–press secretary Sean Spicer stepped up to the podium in the James S. Brady Press Briefing Room for the first time and delivered a statement in which he claimed—no, *insisted*—that the crowd that gathered on the DC mall that Tuesday "was the largest audience to ever witness an inauguration, period, both in person and around the globe."

This was obviously absurd, which probably explained the combative tone. Experts have placed the size of Trump's crowd at about 160,000. Throw in another 20,000 to be generous, and that number is still one-tenth of the estimated 1.8 million who attended President Obama's inauguration in 2009. All you needed was a pair of eyes and photos of the two inaugurations to know that what Sean Spicer was saying was untrue.

Sean and I had been professional acquaintances for years. We'd run into each other in green rooms and at events around DC. I'd always thought of him as a typical Republican press guy: in favor of tax cuts for the wealthy and fewer programs for the poor, not supportive of abortion rights, but not exactly a flame-throwing anti-democracy tyrant. While Sean and I may have disagreed on important issues, we still found a way to talk about our families or topics outside politics while waiting to debate each other on television. Watching his performance that day was jarring. At the State Department, I'd seen hostage videos in which people were forced to say things they didn't want to say. The look in Sean's eyes reminded me of those captives.

Sean was not the first press secretary to be less than honest, intentionally or unintentionally, in a briefing, though his emphatic claim lowered the bar for a first White House press conference. Would he have been better off if he'd stated the obvious truth? Absolutely, when it comes to his reputation. But when it came to the more immediate goal of remaining employed in his position at the time, absolutely not. If he was honest about attendance he would enrage his egomaniacal boss, who would probably mock him and then tell him to clear out his desk.

Maybe Sean figured that if he did this *one* thing, he'd be given leniency to veer toward reality in his subsequent briefings. This would turn out not to be the case; nearly everyone who worked for Trump would get roped into supporting his wild exaggerations and misleading pronouncements. And many of them would be fired anyway.

It's unfortunately true that the perception of your credibility as a speaker can initially be impacted by factors completely out of your control—your age, your gender, your background, your accent, your orientation, your religion, your skin color, your body shape. And there are inherent biases based on all of these factors. As a spokesperson, your credibility is also explicitly influenced by the people you work for, as well as by what that boss allows you to say. It's hard for me not to feel sorry for someone like Sean Spicer, who found himself lying on behalf of his boss, though he should have known what he was getting into.

To his credit, years later Sean wrote in his own book that he "got out of the crowd estimating business a long time ago." A little self-deprecation is always a good tool for owning a mistake.

I've said it is important to practice speeches and presentations so that you sound like yourself when you give them—which may seem paradoxical. But enough preparation is what allows you to be you. Credibility can be similarly hard won. You build credibility over time as part of a team by being hardworking, prepared, respectful of everyone you work with, and curious. Credibility, after all, is a compilation of relationships—the average of how effectively you engage with many different people and audiences. My assessment of Sean Spicer is a good example: while you may have balked that I was (moderately) sympathetic to his position as press secretary for President Trump—shouldn't he have rejected the job offer, if he were truly credible?—it doesn't really matter that I once had pleasant personal conversations with him. He was completely discredited by the way he handled the difficult position he found himself in. While Sean may not have been acting entirely on his own behalf when he was giving his press briefings, he was the one who suffered as a result.

At the same time, I almost always had sympathy for the reporters. Our goals were not the same, but they often overlapped. After all, we were both trying to get information to the American people. As experienced journalists, they knew what my priorities were, and as an experienced communications official, I understood theirs. We could often find common ground. But when I was hired to host a news show on MSNBC it was still a journey to find my own voice after years of speaking on behalf of government officials. One major reason was that the methods of establishing your credibility are radically different in each role.

This shift is difficult for everyone who makes it. A few months after he left his job as the White House press secretary, Robert Gibbs asked me, "When do you think I can be critical of the White House?" It was a tongue in cheek question given I was catching up with him from my West Wing office. But he was getting to the heart of the issue.

"In terms of what?" I half joked. "Do you think anyone in the White House including the president will ever find it acceptable if you are critical?" But of course, that's not what Gibbs was asking. He was asking how to balance his past with his future role, and how to unite the two. When you transition away from the White House, part of your job is to maintain your credibility as the context around you changes dramatically. Because you're no longer speaking on behalf of someone else anymore, you're suddenly faced with the existential question: *What do I think?*

I knew it wouldn't be credible or accurate if I said, "Joe Biden's the most magical unicorn in history and he never makes a mistake!" At the same time, it's important not to be gratuitously critical for the sake of being critical, which some former White House officials do, thinking it will lend them credibility. In reality, it just makes them look like they're trying way too hard to be a contrarian—if the White House and the president are so terrible, why did they work there?

These questions get easier if the administration changes political party; I doubt any former Obama officials had many qualms about criticizing Trump's policies, or lack thereof. Criticizing members of the same party is a more delicate matter. And perhaps the most delicate is the situation I found myself in: the president I'd worked for was still very much in office when I started my new job.

I had to figure out ways to tap into my own experience, both in the administration and beyond it, to explain issues without echoing the Democrats' talking points, or imagining what the president would want me to say in response to certain questions. It wasn't always easy. Like many former administration officials, I'm often asked my opinion as a former senior White House official. I am usually asked some version of the question "What does Joe Biden think?" or "How much of a problem is his age for the Democratic Party?"

At first, it was hard to not automatically regurgitate the kinds of talking points I knew I would have given had I still been in my old job. After all, I'd written many of those talking points. But once I learned, and practiced, the great qualifiers "I haven't worked there in x-number of months," or "This is what is typically going on in a White House at a moment like this," or "If you are sitting in the White House right now you are well aware that public polling shows the American people are concerned about his age. So, the question they are grappling with is what is the most authentic way to deal with that." I could use my experience as an administration official to provide what I hoped was a unique, informed perspective. It was about accepting the reality that I will never not have been Joe Biden's White House press secretary—but also realizing that's not all I would ever be.

6

When to Serve a PsakiBomb

On communicating across divides, at home and with Fox News

On my last day as press secretary, Peter Doocy and I took a photo together that set off a flurry of comments about how short I am (5'3") and how tall he is (6'5").

To this day, the three questions I'm asked most about my time at the White House are: (1) What's Joe Biden really like? (2) Did you get nervous before briefings? (3) How much do you hate Peter Doocy?

For those unfamiliar with a minor subplot of my stint as White House press secretary, Peter Doocy is a White House correspondent for Fox News. Our nearly daily exchanges were often pointed and lengthy, occasionally humorous, and soon enough people came to expect them, which meant they became news items on their own. I had my fans online, just as he had his; they became invested in our contentious briefing room relationship. Conflict is the basis for a lot of TV drama. At some point, someone coined the term "PsakiBomb" and turned it into a hashtag that would trend whenever Peter and I or other reporters in the room had a particularly heated exchange and I'd say something quippy that ended the line of questioning.

My sisters bought "PsakiBomb" sweat shirts—partly out of sisterly pride, and partly to tease me. More than once I showed up on a family Zoom to see them both wearing the sweat shirts.

Peter wasn't the only recipient of these retorts—I had other opportunities to reveal a reporter's perspective to be absurd or irrelevant. For example, when a male reporter from a Catholic news network asked increasingly aggressive questions about Joe Biden's stance on abortion even after I had repeatedly stated his position that he believes it's a woman's right to choose, I finally hit the breaking point and said, "I know you've never faced those choices, nor have you ever been pregnant." It was another way of saying that I knew what he was trying to do with his absurd series of hypotheticals and repetitions of the same points, and I wasn't going to allow it to continue.

But Peter Doocy was my most regular adversary; you could count on him. He was far from the only reporter asking tricky questions—many reporters asked hard questions that dealt with policymaking, and difficult and imperfect policy decisions are made in the White House every day. But Peter's questions had a different tone because they weren't necessarily phrased to get more information, but to prompt a reaction on-camera. Peter didn't entirely have it easy, even among his peers. Because his father, Steve Doocy, has been a mainstay on the *FOX & Friends* morning show since 1998, there were what I considered distracting whisperings about how Peter had landed the plum White

House assignment. He had something to prove. Still, his objective wasn't just to look tough. His job in the briefing room was to push the Fox News agenda, which often meant doing everything he could to challenge the Democratic administration.

What I had to do was manage the back-and-forth in the briefing room, so that my exchanges with Peter would prove at least as beneficial to the White House as they were to Fox. Although we knew the right-wing ecosystem would almost always twist whatever response I gave him into a gaffe that they would use to try to make the Biden administration look inept, petty, cruel, or all of the above, my team and I also got pretty good at predicting what questions Peter might introduce during any given news cycle. We watched a split screen of four channels on the televisions in my office so we could compare Fox's interpretations of the daily news with those of other cable networks, including CNN, MSNBC, and CNBC. We came to learn where they would try to find an opening. And once we could predict their topics, we could plan better answers. We were never going to win over Fox News viewers—this was as likely as Sean Hannity endorsing Joe Biden—but in the briefing room I could refute their arguments with facts, and occasional humor, in order to provide people at home with more details about the president's approach. In doing so, I was also modeling clear, concise talking points for anyone who might find themselves in a similar disagreement with a conservative friend, coworker, or relative. The audience could use my responses to Peter to prepare for their own discussions or debates, and they could even borrow my language (researched, practiced, vetted) verbatim if they wanted.

In his book *Win Every Argument*, journalist Mehdi Hassan writes about the importance of bringing receipts to every debate: "If you're going to win you need to have your damning factual evidence in hand—and you need to be able to deploy it against your opponent in real time."

That tactic came in handy in the briefing room. As gas prices started to rise during the winter of 2022, oil companies tried to pin the blame on the Obama administration's decision not to move forward with the Keystone Pipeline back in 2015. They also blamed the Biden administration for placing limits on drilling. Advocates of fossil fuels argued that there was nothing these companies could do about escalating prices; their hands had been tied by more than one Democratic administration. As "pain at the pump" intensified, conservative websites and Fox News adopted and amplified these false talking points. Cut to the James S. Brady Press Briefing Room:

DOOCY: You guys say all options are on the table. Is restarting Keystone construction one of them?

ME: If we're trying to bring about more supply, that does not address any problem. . . . We're already getting that oil, Peter. The pipeline is just a delivery mechanism. It is not an oil field. So, it does not provide more supply into the system.

The focus on the Keystone Pipeline was a distraction; even if it were approved, the pipeline wouldn't have had an impact on 2022 gas prices because it was years from being operational. Also, it didn't produce oil. And the idea that Biden was preventing drilling was also misguided. At the time, oil companies had nine thousand unused permits on federal land; they weren't even drilling where they had permission. Rather, these companies had chosen *not* to increase drilling because they wanted to maximize profits and reward their shareholders and CEOs.

Did these facts convince Peter Doocy and the Fox viewers to change their position? No, they certainly did not. But even if you can't win—with Fox—preparing straightforward, factual rebuttals to expected challenges may help equip others to make the same counterarguments. Or they can prevent you from resorting to tactics that might give your opponent more ammunition. (If I complained that Doocy was not being fair, for example, he would probably counter that I was whining about fairness because I knew I was in the wrong.) Sometimes the goal is to neuter the argument with a response that can be used to create a more factual, and ultimately winning, narrative in the long run.

Peter was definitely a formidable foe, but I could sometimes use his tactics to my advantage. There was rarely a day when I didn't call on him, in part because ignoring him would have become a talking point for Fox News, and in part because dealing with his questions early on made the rest of the briefing easier. He always started with the most contentious issue, and the more follow-ups he asked, the more facts exposed his often faulty premise.

But while our back-and-forths could be exasperating at times (a nice word for really annoying), the fact is my answer to the question "How much do you hate Peter Doocy?" is, in fact, not at all.

We had light moments in the briefing room, too. When he returned to work after getting married, I made a point to congratulate him. "That's a transcript I can print out and show to my kids one day," he later told the *New York Times*. On my last day, we took a photo together, which we both posted on social media, leading to many conspiracy theories about our height differential including whether I was actually four feet tall and he was seven feet tall. (I am five foot three and he is six foot five.)

When Peter would follow up on a question, or come talk with me in my office when the cameras weren't rolling, he was completely professional, courteous, and reasonable.

These exchanges helped me see him as less of an enemy in the briefing room—even on days when he asked me the most outrageous questions—and more like a fellow human being I had to work with, not against.

This all taught me the importance of connecting in person, even with people who disagree with you. And Peter was far from the only person in the briefing room doing their best to perform for the camera.

This chapter is not specifically about Fox news correspondent Peter Doocy. He's representative of any person in your life who challenges you: publicly or privately, fairly or unfairly. Your Peter Doocy might be someone at work who always corrects you during meetings, or a close family member who confronts you with an opposing view and makes you feel uncomfortable. Unlike Peter Doocy himself, who was doing his job (and we don't have enough time in this book for a full psycho-analysis of what it must be like to work at Fox News), your Peter Doocy might not even be doing it on purpose.

The first thing to remember about communicating across divides—whether political or personal—is that it takes courage, and courage is something you can learn. When I was growing up, my parents, and especially my dad, pushed us to try new things. Summer vacations were a marathon: He would wake us around 6:00 a.m. to make sure we were ready for a packed day of strenuous physical activity. We took long mountain bike rides up and down the winding roads of Vermont. An eight-hour canoe trip became an annual tradition starting when my sister and I were as young as seven and five. When I was four, my dad picked me up from the side of a pool, held me in his arms while we climbed to the top of the high dive, and jumped.

So, I was prepared, one winter, when I found myself sitting next to my dad on a chairlift that would drop us at the top of a mountain in Vermont. It was cold and windy; visibility was, I'm sure, poor. My dad told me that he expected me to ski down on my own. I was scared. But I felt a rush of determination when we pushed off the lift. After some heart-racing moments skidding on the ice, I made it all the way down—full of adrenaline, and no broken bones. Neither of my parents acknowledged that there was anything out of the ordinary about this occasion. Did I mention I was five?

My dad's intensity made family vacations more of a test of endurance than a restful break, but these moments gave me the confidence to navigate intimidating and even scary challenges for the rest of my life. I'm grateful to him because now, for me, fear is a reason *to* do something, not avoid it. Challenging yourself—physically, intellectually, professionally, and personally—is one of the best ways to grow. Once you get over the fear, you may realize that you actually can ski down the mountain—or run the meeting, speak at a conference, or broach an awkward topic. And my dad always told me that if you aren't a little nervous about a new job you might be overqualified for it. Shorthand: always take the leap, even when you're scared.

My dad is also a voracious consumer of news, and as you'd expect, his response to the demands of my job is not about fear, but frustration. A former real estate developer in his early eighties, he used to be a Republican, in an old-school, "fiscal conservative" way. He'd say that what ultimately steered him toward the Democrats was the 2000 election of George W. Bush because he felt like the party was becoming more socially conservative than he was. Over the years, he's transformed into a progressive Democrat. He spends hours yelling at cable news hosts (maybe even at me) every week; an evening with him usually entails at least one expletive-laden rant about the misguided actions of one politician or another. It's entirely possible to get up from the dinner table, use the restroom, refill your wineglass, and return to find my dad still delivering his monologue about his disgust with the man from Mar-a-Lago. "I could never do your job," he'd say to me during my first months as press secretary. "I would just want to rip their heads off." His targets were many; he meant, at various points, the reporters who'd ask obtuse questions, the members of Congress who were hard to convince of sensible legislation, and the cable news anchors who would put me through the wringer when I went on their shows.

One of the great things about becoming an adult is getting to see your parents as human beings. Here is where, in exchange for all the bravery my dad taught me as a child, I have something to teach him about communication. "The thing is," I'd reply, "yelling doesn't really work. That's not what I do. It's not about who talks louder or even who has the last word—it's about convincing them to listen to what you have to say."

In some ways, this might seem like setting a low bar. Isn't effective communication about more than just convincing people to *listen*? Isn't it about convincing them that you're right? In an era of polarization and closed minds, if a communications strategy doesn't change opinions or at least build support it's hard to see how it even matters.

But before someone can change their mind, they have to be willing to first even consider an alternative position. Trying to verbally force your viewpoint on someone who doesn't share it is a recipe for failure—especially when your views diverge. It puts the other person on the defensive, hardening their position. If you want true, long-term agreement, you need to create the conditions for everyone to feel that the choice of what to believe is their own.

To use another metaphor: Successful communication is sometimes about building a bridge where there wasn't one before. Sometimes all you need is a footbridge to traverse a stream. Sometimes you need a suspension bridge that spans miles and miles. That requires much more planning, effort, and resources to build. Of course, it's great if the person on the other side just walks (or drives) across; that's always the hope. But they first need to see the bridge, and then determine for themselves that the structure is sturdy enough to support both of you.

Going door to door campaigning in Iowa in my twenties, I learned that successful communication involved much more than knowing what to say and how to say it. The first step was about being brave enough to knock, not knowing what response you'll get, and having the confidence to know that whatever's on the other side, you can build a bridge to get there. Sometimes engaging doesn't work the first time and you have to fine-tune your message based on what you hear and try again (and again) to connect.

Building bridges can be even more intimidating today. But one of the biggest communication mistakes people make is to discount the enormous rewards that can come from connecting with an audience that may not want to engage. In an age of cultural, political, and personal polarization, we tend to think of engagement as a contest—on social media, the term "engagement" refers to the quantifiable "likes," views, and reposts a missive might collect. The function of communication has been reduced to winning and losing: the goal of any post or comment is either to join a sea of like-minded people drowning out voices we don't approve of, or to convince the other side to join us, *urgently*.

The exchanges taking place in these digital ecosystems may create a forum for everyone to successfully share information and opinions, but they aren't models for effective communication. By discouraging in-person interaction, social media platforms make it easy to be harsh and divisive. On most platforms, any form of compromise or finding common ground is usually foreclosed after a few barbs back and forth. The relentless pace of online news means no one feels they have or need the time to form a nuanced opinion. Fake news and unconfirmed stories—from dramatic celebrity gossip to conspiracy theories—multiply, and they're way more exciting to read than a news story on budget reconciliation. (Still too complicated to explain here.) Given that time is precious, and stakes can be high—or at least feel high—why would anyone waste hours trying to patiently show a member of the other side where they might reconsider their views? They could just collect online approval from people who already agree with them.

But you might first consider whether you aren't also wasting your time if you're only ever "preaching to the choir," as the saying goes. Putting people in rigid categories can generate feelings of inclusion and exclusion, which further exacerbate the problem. In his book, *Belonging*, the psychologist Geoffrey L. Cohen proposes that "belonging isn't a by-product of success but a condition for it—in school, work, home, healthcare settings, negotiations, politics, community policing, and virtually every domain in which humans deal with humans." Feeling a genuine connection to others is vital to successful communication, and successful communication makes everyone involved feel like they are part of something bigger than themselves—even if it's just a group of two. When you engage in a way that makes your audience feel they are being welcomed into your circle, they're more willing to give you a chance, listen to you, and entertain the idea that what you have to say is important to them. The further you push them away, however, the more likely they are to not only resent you but also consider your message harmful: threatening to everything they believe.

For a classic example of how political polarization can demolish reason, let's go back to the debate about Obamacare. In that case, the core principle of the Affordable Care Act—to provide universal healthcare coverage—didn't come out of progressive lobbyists or recommendations from liberal economists. It came from the Heritage Foundation, one of the most influential think tanks on the right wing. Their proposal was first tested on a smaller scale by Mitt Romney in Massachusetts, to great success. Once Barack Obama decided to make it the centerpiece of his healthcare reform plan, the conservatives who'd been thumbs up were immediately thumbs down. The framing of the policy suddenly changed—not because the policy itself had changed in any substantial way, but because of who was advocating for it. The flip was so dramatic that even the Heritage Foundation itself started criticizing the policy it had come up with in the first place. (Romney, as I said earlier, also turned against it.)

Our team accepted that in order for enough people to embrace the benefits of Obamacare, to see it as an essential part of their lives, we couldn't jam President Obama's affiliation with it down their throats. (In a memorable segment on Jimmy Kimmel's late-night show, interviewees repeatedly said they didn't like Obamacare but did like the ACA, unaware that they were the same thing.) We took a more measured approach by pulling out the components that people loved, the elements of the policy that both sides of the aisle could agree on. The ability to keep your children on your health insurance until they were twenty-six saved everyone money and stress. Protecting people with preexisting conditions from being dropped by their insurance was important for people of all class backgrounds, regardless of party affiliation. Over time, popular views changed. Not that deep-red states developed an appreciation for Obama, but they came to recognize that the bill was helping people. As the popularity of ACA benefits grew, so did approval of the president's handling of healthcare.

My point in talking about the ACA again is that a divide can be defined not by something you did, or believe, but by the box your audience has put you in, regardless of the truth of your message or your own ability to deliver it. And while this is particularly problematic in politics, it goes well beyond that sphere. Especially in this moment, when attention spans are a sliver of their former selves, it can seem almost revolutionary to try to understand each other without resorting to one-dimensional labels and brands.

All this makes establishing and maintaining your credibility even more important. As scary as the snap toxicity of online "debate" is, if you can find and focus on your primary audience (and not an amorphous, digital amoeba like Facebook or Instagram), you can enhance your credibility, push back against those who wish to define you, and create space for authentic and successful engagement. Connecting with people, whether they're inclined to agree with you or not, works best when you meet them where they are. Are they skeptical? Are they uninterested? Are they intrigued but don't have enough information? Starting your entreaty with something sympathetic like "I know you may think we don't agree on everything, but . . ." will go a long way to building trust.

I worry about how damaging social media and their algorithms are to civil discourse. These platforms warrant reforms and accountability that will require action at both the state and federal levels. It would be wise to avoid them altogether, but that's not really an option if you're trying to speak to a broad range of people. These forums reach millions, and it's essential not to give up the playing field when you're trying to communicate. That's why I didn't ignore Fox News. Just the opposite. Of all the Sunday show appearances I did during my time at the White House, I appeared on *Fox News Sunday* more than any other Sunday show. Engaging broadly means I left myself open to more public attacks, by individuals, organizations, and even countries (we'll get to that later in the book), but walking away from talking to anyone I disagreed with wasn't an option.

I have frequently had Republicans on my show on MSNBC. Not to performatively debate them, though I will definitely push back on inaccurate statements, but because I see it as an important part of viewers understanding what is happening in Washington, in politics, and in global events.

Learning to both tolerate and overcome discomfort is necessary for any deep, meaningful relationship. Even when being battered and bruised online, on air, and in person in my job, I always believed there was some chance of engagement, or hope for connection—not with everyone, and in some cases with only a small subset of an audience that was previously hostile—if I could figure out how to find it.

Closer to home, my abiding hope for connection helped me understand when to attempt to engage and when to hold back with one of my relatives. My uncle Bob, who passed away from cancer back in 2009, was a retired New York City police officer—a Fox News–loving conservative who was in a constant state of eye roll at the rest of our family's progressive politics. We loved him. And we strongly disagreed with him on just about everything.

My mom seemed to have an intuitive protocol in place about when and how to talk to him, and as we got older, my sisters and I followed her lead. If he said something about a politician or issue we cared about, but in a relatively calm or friendly tone, we might respond, "Come on, Uncle Bob, you don't really believe that, do you?" In more heated exchanges, my mother would sometimes respond bluntly: "That is just not true." There were even a few times when she pulled him aside because she didn't want him to repeat what he had said, or when she didn't want us to hear what she was about to say to him.

But we never had screaming political debates over the dinner table, because that wouldn't have made a damn bit of difference to either side. This rule has stuck with me. While it doesn't happen often, occasionally I'll find myself at a restaurant, or a baseball game, or in the airport, when someone decides they want to walk up and tell me how much they disagree with me. I love a good debate, but I'm not interested in debating in these settings, particularly because I can almost always tell within a few seconds that the person who thinks it's a good idea to approach a stranger and attack her political beliefs is not a person who is open to bridging a gap. Instead, I respond, "Thanks for sharing with me," or, "All right, I guess we disagree." There's no point in debating someone who just wants to debate—particularly when you're about to miss a plane or lose your place in line for a hot dog.

* * *

To be an effective communicator, you don't have to be the loudest person in a room. You don't have to get in the last word, or the most words, during a disagreement to change minds. In fact, that's probably a bad strategy. The best communication offers both explanation and empathy and generates both understanding and curiosity. It means convincing a specific person or group that they should at least consider your points as they make a decision—whether it's about a candidate, a product, or a big personal change. Communication is about adapting your approach when needed, thinking hard about how your information or opinion might be received, and, at times, being fearless.

So how do you build a bridge? Let's assume you've done your homework and you know your audience: it's a tough crowd. A major overture to move your doubtful conversation partner in a different direction probably won't work. Instead, little nudges toward connection can help make uncomfortable conversations more manageable.

There are many subtle strategies you can use to encourage your audience to hear you out. Speaking humbly about hardships can create a narrative bond that transcends (at least for a moment) more fundamental divisions. Losing a family member, struggling to put food on the table, personal failures—these are the sorts of stories that can humanize someone you may have otherwise seen one-dimensionally. George W. Bush talking about his struggles with alcohol, Bill Clinton talking about losing a parent as a child, Barack Obama talking about life after his father abandoned him: in these moments, we see glimpses of the person behind the presidential seal. There may be no more powerful example than when Joe Biden talks about losing his wife and daughter in a car accident, and one of his sons to brain cancer. But it also doesn't have to be a narrative involving suffering to have transcendent power: Jimmy Carter's indisputably profound religious faith made him a role model for many who might have otherwise thought little of him.

One of my favorite ways to connect across divides is to present myself as flawed. And guess what? We all are. There's nothing a skeptical audience hates more than someone who thinks she's better than everyone else. Acknowledging your imperfections with humor, and laughing at yourself, can help bring down guards. But it can be easy to hit an off note, so you'll definitely want to work out your self-deprecating comments in advance (though you don't want that preparation to show—a skeptical audience also hates inauthenticity). If the subject is military aid to Ukraine, mentioning my inability to safely ride a bicycle (sad but true) would come off as not only completely random but also incredibly self-obsessed. But if we're talking about how the infrastructure bill is going to build wider roads, my two-wheel travails might actually work.

Humor that's not self-effacing can also work. Not only is there evidence that we remember information better when it makes us laugh, but also it's hard not to recognize that you have something in common when the other person is laughing just as hard as you are. Stanford's Naomi Bagdonas, who has written extensively on humor as a business tool, has a favorite example of this, which, as it happens, I worked on behind the scenes. At one point during his 2011 State of the Union address, President Obama mentioned, "The Interior Department is in charge of salmon while they're in fresh water, but the Commerce Department handles them when they're in salt water. And I hear it gets even more complicated once they're smoked." It seemed to be the kind of joke that only Washington could love, but when NPR asked its listeners the next day which three words stood out most from Obama's speech, "once they're smoked" was the runaway winner. "What was fascinating about this is it held true across political affiliation as well," Bagdonas points out.

That fact reveals something very clever about Obama's joke (which, you can probably guess, was not made up on the spot). Given the right's stereotypes about Democrats, the president couldn't simply say in his speech that he was against what he saw as overregulation—even though he was. Half the country would brush it off as a lie told in service of tricking them into thinking he's on their side and convincing them to vote for him when he was up for reelection the next year. Obama instead picked a tangible example of overregulation—it's a lot easier to visualize a fish than a carbon credit—and described it with humor, which demonstrated that he not only understood conservatives' concern with overregulation but also could empathize with someone who holds that view. Many of those who were chuckling were the sorts of people who spent the rest of their political bandwidth trying to oppose everything President Obama was in favor of. But the laugh may have made a few of them just a tiny bit more open-minded. He couldn't have won over his audience with facts alone; he knew he had to make an emotional connection. Just make sure, if you go in for the joke, it's actually funny.

7

A Punch Line China Would Find Funny

On making mistakes, issuing clarifications,
correcting yourself, and apologizing

No joking around on busy news days, which required a pretty stern management of the questioning.

It took one day on the job as White House press secretary for me to have to clarify a comment—I hadn't adequately expressed the president's confidence in the FBI director in my first briefing—and less than two weeks to make a clumsy statement at the podium that required an apology. On February 2, 2021, I was asked a pretty straightforward question about "whether the president has made a decision on keeping, or keeping the scope of, Space Force."

The Space Force (USSF) is the newest of the six branches of the military, established during the final year of the Trump administration. During our first twelve days in the White House, the topic hadn't come up in discussions, which were laser-focused on the COVID vaccine rollout and passing legislation to help turn around the economy. When I heard the reporter's question, the first thing that came to mind was the satirical TV show *Space Force*, starring Steve Carell.

"Wow. Space Force," I replied, breaking into a smile. The reporter didn't get why I was smiling.

"It's an entire military branch," he said in a scolding tone.

I quickly regained my composure. "I am happy to check with our Space Force point of contact," I said. "I'm not sure who that is. I will find out and see if we have any update on that."

I didn't take the question seriously enough, which I would soon regret. Conservative pundits criticized my dismissive tone, and a couple of Republican Congress members seized the opportunity to grandstand. One called my comments "disrespectful." Another said I'd turned our military into "a punch line" that "China would find funny." That clearly had not been my intention. Though it has a funny name if your association is Steve Carell, the Space Force was established to reinvigorate the Air Force's legacy space organizations; its responsibilities include monitoring space debris, overseeing military and GPS satellites, and making plans for possible future military operations beyond the Earth's atmosphere. Trump's aggressive and—if I may say so—corny branding campaign for the Space Force, which included a lot of merch, did no favors for these serious operations, and the people who serve them. Of all the wild and crazy aspects of the Trump legacy, I had not paid the Space Force much attention before that day, so I wasn't aware of the history and purpose of the office.

I had made a mistake. I knew the president wanted me to present a serious and calm tone at the briefings, and I had unintentionally dismissed an important division of the military and given conservatives justification to criticize me and the administration. I was embarrassed that I'd created a distraction from the administration's policies and goals, mad at myself, and also a little annoyed by the overreaction.

My friend and press office colleague Karine Jean-Pierre gave me a Space Force T-shirt to make me feel better—a great example of communicating through humor. The gesture acknowledged my frustration while also putting the situation in perspective. But I knew I needed to fix my mistake before it became an even bigger story. Speed and sincerity are key when you're apologizing, so the next day I posted on Twitter: "We look forward to the continuing work of Space Force and invite the members of the team to come visit us in the briefing room anytime to share an update on their important work." It didn't matter. The next morning, *FOX & Friends* cohost Brian Kilmeade called my tweet "a sarcastic comment" and then tried to prove his point by reading it on air in a cartoonishly sycophantic voice. I'd learned the lesson over and over while at State, but here it was again: when your audience is extremely combative, it sometimes doesn't matter what you say; if detractors can't twist your words, they'll twist your intention.

Still, I needed to correct the record for anyone actually interested in the White House's perspective. At the next briefing, the subject of support for Space Force was raised again. This time, I answered with complete seriousness: "They absolutely have the full support of the Biden administration, and we are not revisiting the decision to establish the Space Force. The desire for the Department of Defense to focus greater attention and resources on the growing security challenges in space has long been a bipartisan issue informed by numerous independent commissions and studies conducted across multiple administrations. And thousands of men and women proudly serve in the Space Force."

A few days later, one of the leaders of the Space Force sent me a note to tell me there were no hard feelings. I was profoundly impressed by the elegance of the response: that he took the time to quickly extend a little reassurance said just as much as his actual note did. His grace and good humor helped me feel better about my gaffe. He also gifted me with a Space Force pin, which I kept as a reminder of not only his classy reaction but also the importance of taking every question seriously, even the ones that sound silly on the surface.

We all screw up once in a while . . . or every day. Although not all my mistakes have caused days of Twitter fighting and inspired conservative media to question my allegiance to the United States, there's rarely been a day in my career that I didn't wish I'd answered a question with greater clarity or given more context. What I came to realize is that fixing mistakes is not something you have to do because you're bad at your job, but because it is a part of your job. Doing it well means you're doing your job well; the solution to poorly communicating something the first time is not to stop communicating, but to keep communicating.

There are times for funny and even flippant responses in public and in private, and there are times when revealing authentic emotion can be a crucial bridge to engagement. But these moments should be chosen carefully; successfully landing a joke requires an audience willing to engage with it, and emotions can get the better of you. I learned this the hard way more than once: frustration, annoyance, and even occasional anger aren't usually helpful when you're trying to get a message across; the only message they really send is that you're frustrated, annoyed, or angry, and people don't like to be on the receiving end of any of that. If some of the mistakes I've made during my career were the result of simply speaking too soon or failing to ask the right questions (like when I denied John Kerry was on his yacht in Nantucket during a military coup), the blunders I've learned the most from came from my inability to keep my feelings in check, whether they stemmed from my need to impress someone or just good old-fashioned exasperation.

In December 2021, as people prepared to travel for their first real holidays since the onset of the pandemic in March 2020, the demand for COVID tests spiked. There simply weren't enough available for the huge numbers of American people who wanted and needed them. I came to the briefing room prepared to lay out what steps the administration had taken to speed up manufacturing and make tests more readily available to the public. I was experiencing this shortage like everyone else who couldn't find enough tests, as I, too, was preparing for the holidays, with lots of family visiting, but I was also dealing with it as a White House staffer who understood how difficult it was to accurately anticipate the demand for tests during this once-in-a-lifetime pandemic. (I understood this because I sat in hours of meetings about it.) Our answers weren't great because there were no great answers yet ("not a comms problem" comes to mind). But some of the questioning was so repetitive and relentless it eventually wore me down.

One of the things that has changed about press briefings in the era of YouTube and Twitter is that every outlet, from print to television, wants to get a clip of their reporter asking the big question of the day. This means that a briefing can be like listening to a song on repeat; each reporter asks a question and gets an answer, and then the next reporter asks the same question and gets the same answer, and the next, and the next, ad nauseam. And since each reporter wants to show their viewers that they're tough and not afraid to ask the hard questions, not only are they asking the same thing, but also they might put their identical questions forward in an exaggerated, aggressive way. Some days I had to draw on all my self-control not to get into an argument, or even just a tiff, with these reporters. My predecessors in the role can relate. "On the rare occasions when the briefing was getting too intense or testy and a reporter was showing off for the cameras," former press secretary Dana Perino writes in her book *And the Good News Is . . .* , "I'd just rest my hand next to my water, out of view of anyone, keep a pleasant look on my face, and flip 'em the bird." I'm kind of surprised I never thought to do that.

On this day in December, I'd walked through every step we'd taken to increase COVID testing, over and over again. NPR reporter Mara Liasson returned to the subject. Why wasn't the administration using countries like the United Kingdom as models and sending rapid tests to anyone who asked for them? she asked.

I was exhausted and exasperated. I shot back in a sarcastic tone, "Should we just send one to every American?"

I rewatched a clip of this moment recently, and my performance has not improved with age. As soon as I said the words, I wished I had a clicker to go back five seconds. People who have been in accidents often describe a sense that the world has slowed down and their perception of what's going on has become unforgettably detailed. That's a bit like how it was for me up on the podium that day; even now, I remember what dress I was wearing—and not just because my mistake played repeatedly on cable and social media platforms. (Short sleeves, black and white, bold geometric print.)

As soon as my response went public, I became a target for Americans' frustration and disappointment about the pandemic and the government's handling of it; I hadn't just irritated conservatives, but supporters of the president, who also couldn't find tests anywhere. And I understood why. To start with, I had not even answered the focused question she asked. It didn't matter that at that moment, when tests were already low in supply, it would have been a terrible, impractical, and impossible idea to send out 300 million of them to Americans; an estimated half would have been discarded. Even when we did make free tests available, only about 20 percent of the public took advantage of the offer, leaving tens of thousands of tests at risk of expiring. But just as my response had been emotional, so, too, was the public's. That wasn't their fault—successful communication requires you to validate your audience's relationship to the issue at hand. The public was dependent on the administration to get them access to tests, and on me not to give insensitive responses to questions people were asking. My exasperation at having to talk about a situation in which there were no easy solutions should have taken a back seat, or better, gotten out of the car.

It didn't matter that I was right about the recklessness of sending out all those test kits; I still had to eat crow on this one. At the podium the next day I acknowledged my mistake. "There's not a day that goes by that I don't leave this podium and wish I would have said something with greater context or more precision or additional information," I said. (Sound familiar?) "And that day there was a lot of good questioning on testing. And during that briefing I conveyed a lot of information about our expansion of testing, about the 50 million tests that we were making available, about the twenty thousand free testing sites. And I should have included that additional context again in that answer, yes. Going back, I wish I would have done that." I then went on to offer details about the free tests that we were making available for those who asked for them and reinforced the president's commitment to improving our COVID response.

Was I immediately forgiven for my comment? Of course not. But I'd known I wouldn't be. I *was* surprised by some of the gleeful responses to my screw-up, as if my temporary lapse in patience was reason to celebrate. Nevertheless, this was an opportunity to both correct the record and bolster my credibility by being honest about my mistake.

It was also a lesson in the importance of finding a way to emotionally cope with the repetition that can happen in press conferences, or in any situation where you have to communicate information that might be repetitive to you but is vital to your audience. From then on, I started to play a guessing game with my team about how many identical questions the reporters in the briefing room would ask about a particular topic on any given day. I would always put the first bet on the table.

During the spring of 2022, a number of prominent officials, including Speaker of the House Nancy Pelosi, tested positive for COVID. At the time, the Centers for Disease Control had a confusing definition of what was considered "a close contact," and there was an (understandable) obsession with whether the president might have been exposed. There were going to be endless stories about the possibility.

"So how many questions are we going to get today about whether or not Speaker Pelosi was a 'close contact' of President Biden's?" I asked the team while flipping through my briefing book. "I'm betting nine. Anyone else?"

Kevin Munoz, our spokesperson on COVID response, jumped in with fifteen. Chris Meagher, a tall, genial deputy press secretary who is an eternal optimist, guessed it would end at five. I won; it was around ten.

Sometimes you can quickly overcome a mistake with honesty and humility; other times the grace and forgiveness of those who saw you mess up really help. In our age of digital communication, I am far from the only person who regrets what I've written in an email. I should have learned my lesson in 2003 when I was an aspiring press aide working for the Kerry campaign in Iowa and volunteered to take on more responsibilities. It was early in the primary season and the national campaign hadn't yet hired more seasoned staff to serve as the communications and media experts on the ground. My duties included updating Robert Gibbs, who would later become my boss and good friend but was at the time the campaign communications director, on what the Iowa press corps was regularly asking and reporting. Gibbs was already a larger-than-life political communications guru who had worked for the Democratic Senatorial Campaign Committee before taking on the job as the communications director for the leading presidential candidate on the Democratic side. I wanted to impress him.

One day that summer, I heard from a few reporters who were looking for a response that Vermont governor Howard Dean was about to run his first paid TV ads. This was a pretty big development at the time; most campaigns didn't have enough money for TV ads that early in the election cycle. To me, it was evidence that the Dean campaign, which was ahead in Iowa at the time, was betting big by spending to define their candidate early—and even potentially define his opponents. If he was successful, he might further lock up the caucus vote and turn his focus to New Hampshire. Since he was from the neighboring state, he might already have preemptive momentum there. None of that was great news if you were working for a candidate running against him.

Excited about providing the big boss with this information, I sent Gibbs an email about the intel on the advertising buys. He replied thanking me, and we went back and forth over email about the Dean campaign and what was happening on the ground in Iowa. At some point, he asked which reporters had asked about the Dean ad buys. In an effort not to forget a single reporter's name, I pulled up the Iowa press list in my cc: line. I was planning to copy the relevant addresses, paste them into my email, pick out the relevant names, delete the cc:, and hit "send." Remember this was 2003; email hadn't been around *that* long, so I thought this was a fairly slick move. Except, eager to show Gibbs how efficient I was, I skipped that "delete" step. The entire Iowa press corps received an email from me a few seconds later. Well, not just one email. A whole string of emails, in which Gibbs and I were making jokes about Dean's candidacy, which was something the Kerry campaign would never have wanted the press corps to see.

Immediately, with a sinking feeling in my stomach, I realized what I'd done. I was surely going to get fired.

Regardless of my fate, I knew I couldn't just pretend it didn't happen—that would allow the mistake to snowball. As nerve-racking as it was, I immediately called Gibbs—since I was so many rungs below him, we'd never met in person—to prevent him from replying.

Fortunately, he didn't freak out. He kind of laughed and told me to keep track of anyone who asked me about our email exchange.

Next I needed to explain to John Norris, the Iowa state director and my direct boss, that I'd criticized the campaign of one of Senator Kerry's top opponents in front of reporters when our goal was to stay above the fray. Soft-spoken and likable, Norris was the well-respected former chief of staff to Iowa's Democratic governor; he only raised his voice when he had reached a real point of exasperation. I was fairly certain this would be one of those times. I walked into his office, looked around, and was confused—he wasn't at his desk, so where . . . ?

Then I spotted him, lying on the floor to stretch his back, taking a break from the combined stress of leading the campaign and waiting for the birth of his first kids, twins. I hated to add to his stress, but to my surprise, he also responded calmly. He had me walk through exactly what happened and asked if anyone had called for comment or to follow up. Somehow no one had—or even replied to the email. I was starting to wonder if I had just imagined my blunder.

Later that night, after the dust had settled, I went to an event with Senator Kerry and was hanging out near the press file, the area where the press write their reports. Mike Glover, an old-school chain-smoking AP reporter, walked over to me.

"So, you should know, Jen, you put all of us on that email chain you had with Gibbs," he said gently.

"Yeah, that wasn't a high point of my day," I replied. "Clearly, I didn't intend to share that note and I regretted it immediately."

"I know," he said. Then he walked away.

Mike never wrote about the email, and no one brought it up to me again. I don't know if that was because there were so many other news stories happening or because people in Iowa are just nicer than most and they took pity on a young staffer like me, but that day taught me a few lessons. Mistakes are going to happen in any fast-paced industry. I confessed to my bosses immediately, which is exactly what you should do when you mess up. As embarrassing as it can be to botch something, everyone around you will be doubly upset if your mistake is compounded because they didn't know about it and kept operating as if it hadn't happened. Nobody likes to have to mop up after someone else, but what they like even less is having to do it when the mess has spread without them knowing.

My frantic call to Gibbs still looms large in my memory. Recently, I asked him what he was thinking on his end of the conversation. Had I actually been close to losing my job? He laughed and said he didn't even remember that day.

You'd think that after this scare I would have begun a new phase of being very, very careful around all electronic communications. Well, not quite. Sometimes I think the internet has only multiplied the ways we can go wrong.

As the deputy White House press secretary in 2009, I was responsible for all incoming questions about economic issues. Because we were in a financial crisis, this meant spending a lot of time on the phone with the Treasury Department, which played an enormous role in managing the government's response.

President Obama had just named lawyer Ken Feinberg as the special master for executive compensation, which meant he would determine how much the CEOs of the companies the government had assisted in bailing out could get paid—a controversial move, because it gave the government a role in determining the limitations of private sector pay packages. While the public was outraged by the reckless behavior on Wall Street, introducing Feinberg in this position was a move that put more stress on the growing tension between the White House and the business community (and their Republican supporters). The announcement of the "compensation czar" was a huge story.

Feinberg technically worked at the Treasury Department, who told us they were planning to do just three interviews with the major broadcast networks—ABC, CBS, and NBC—in order to get the message about Feinberg's appointment out to a broad audience. Unsurprisingly, other media organizations started calling senior members of the economic team to voice their displeasure at this perceived injustice. We added interviews with Bloomberg News and CNBC.

Then Fox News complained. Actually, they did more than complain. Despite the fact that they hadn't even requested an interview, they accused the administration of excluding them. We added an interview with one of their anchors, but the network's handling of the situation was just another interaction with Fox that left a bad taste in my mouth. They continued to complain even after the interview was confirmed, did not handle the interview or reporting fairly in my view, and conveniently forgot that they had never even requested an interview, so we had actually helped them out by scheduling one.

After a long day of dealing with all this, I vented on an email chain with my friends at the Treasury Department. "I am putting some dead fish in the Fox cubby," I joked, alluding to the time when Rahm Emanuel sent a dead fish to a pollster who'd made him unhappy. Such "dead fish" references were a well-known running gag among Obama staff; on Rahm's last day at the White House, Austan Goolsbee, the Council of Economic Advisers chair, gifted his old friend a dead carp. I also sent some frustrated notes to my colleagues about the Feinberg coverage, adding: "bret baier just did a stupid piece on it—but he is a lunatic."

Any email between the White House and a government agency is subject to a FOIA (Freedom of Information Act) request, which allows outside organizations like news outlets or watchdog groups to petition to read it. When the right-wing organization Judicial Watch filed a FOIA request for all the email exchanges around Feinberg's appointment in 2010, my harsh note about Bret Baier was among those that were made public.

While my comments about Fox and its anchors were far from the most contemptuous unearthed by Judicial Watch, I was mortified. There were plenty of fair criticisms to make against the content aired on Fox News and how they engaged with the White House, but my personal attack on Baier was unwarranted and I definitely should have known better than to vent on my White House email. When I reread my email distanced from the heat of the moment, I cringed and thought about what my mother would say. She wasn't a fan of Fox News, but she wouldn't have wanted me to speak about anyone that way. I emailed Bret immediately and apologized.

I wrote something like, I know we don't know each other, but that is not how I typically handle things.

I didn't expect a reply. But not only did he respond; he invited me to lunch. Once again, I found myself bowled over by someone's ability to communicate goodwill in a quick note. A few days later, we met at a restaurant down the street from the White House and talked about our families, his kids, and my recent wedding.

I would continue to take issue with the way Fox News reported stories in the years ahead, but in the back of my mind I remembered Bret's very kind—and opposite of lunatic—handling of what had been a nasty, personal attack. His response has stuck with me during moments when I have dealt with people, professionally or personally, who have made comments about me publicly or privately that were inaccurate or unfair. Sometimes the lesson you learn from your own mistake comes from a surprising source.

* * *

I've been making mistakes for most of my life—I'm pretty experienced at it. One of the first times I can remember committing what we could call a gaffe was when I was around eleven years old. I was having dinner with my friend's family, and we were talking about sports. "I would never want to play hockey," I said. "You could lose all your teeth!"

I'm also experienced in receiving kind responses to my mistakes that made it easier for me to acknowledge them. That night, my friend's dad smiled. "Well, I played hockey. . . . And I did lose many of my teeth!" His combination of tact and humor allowed me to quickly apologize, and to learn a valuable lesson: think before you speak, because you never know a person's full history or circumstances. The grace that he and many others have shown me has stuck with me as a guide for how to behave when people make mistakes—whether at work, among friends, or anywhere.

More than once I have had to quickly cover up someone's unintentional admission in front of my young kids that the tooth fairy or other magical childhood figure does not exist. And in those moments, my audience is not the friend or neighbor who has put their foot in their mouth and unintentionally ruined the magic, but my child. So instead of nodding along with the adult, I launch into a complicated explanation that goes something like this: "Well, Mary [it isn't always a Mary] probably doesn't remember what happens when you lose a tooth, because she lost her last one so many years ago. But next time you lose a tooth and the tooth fairy brings you something, we'll have to make sure we tell Mary all about it." Mary may look at me like I'm crazy, but in the moment I don't care, because my goal is to salvage the tooth fairy's reputation with my kids.

Mary, too, is my audience, just not primary. I'm letting her know that I wish she hadn't exposed the truth in front of my child, and that in the future she should be more aware of whom she's speaking to and what their needs might be. I'm sending a signal about who is in charge of explaining the world to my children. But I'm also sending a signal that I'm not so upset as to make a big a deal out of it. In fact, I've worded my response so that the criticism of Mary is not about something she did, but something that happened to her: her fading memory. I've framed her as a sympathetic figure. I've also given her a graceful off-ramp by providing her with an excuse. Instead of being annoyed with me, she's more likely to be mildly grateful, or at least neutral. I've proposed an overarching objective (don't take away the innocence of this child just yet) that Mary could agree to without having to abandon her underlying lack of faith in the tooth fairy. If successful in all this, I will have transformed a potentially unreceptive secondary audience into my ally in engaging the primary one. In this instance, that alliance was especially important, because I was breaking a central rule of successful communication, which was that I wasn't telling the truth. With kids, there can sometimes be room for the white lie.

And if you still believe that the tooth fairy is real, I apologize for my bad memory. It's a very important branch of the military.

8

Kindergarten Open House on the Worst Day in the White House

*On saying no, explaining your boundaries,
and knowing how to quit*

Outside my West Wing office with nine-month-old Vivi,
whom I needed to pick up early from daycare that day. I
enlisted my colleagues to help babysit. It takes a village!

When you're a working parent, personal responsibilities can
sometimes challenge your ability to be in the room for important discussions at work, and you have to learn how to manage your
priorities—and depend on other people to help you out. The morning of August 26, 2021, I walked into the Situation Room for our

scheduled presidential briefing. It was just five days before the deadline
to withdraw all troops from Afghanistan after a twenty-year-long war.
Every day felt like borrowed time. Threats of a potential terrorist attack
multiplied, as did the large crowd gathered outside the Kabul airport
hoping to leave the country.

August had already been a heartbreaking month. Stories about chaos
at the airport dominated the airwaves. A photo of a young Afghan man
hanging from the wing of a plane taking off showed the desperation of
people who wanted to flee the Taliban regime. The mood that morning
was somber, but that had been the mood for a while. I whispered to the
deputy national security advisor, Jon Finer, that I thought we had made
progress in helping some reporters better understand the seriousness of
the threats. His response caught me off guard.

"There was an attack this morning," he whispered.

I quickly found my seat on the back bench. This is just what it
sounds like: You may have seen photos of the Situation Room, with
the table in the middle where officials sit. Their staffers sit behind
them in chairs that line the back of the room in order to pass them
notes, or offer help if they need it. When the president, the commander in chief, entered the Situation Room, everyone stood. Military leadership gave an update from the ground on what we knew
about the explosion outside the airport's Abbey Gate. At first, there
were four casualties. As the meeting proceeded, the number of those
gravely injured began to rise. Eventually, we would learn that the
blast killed 13 US troops and an estimated 170 Afghans. As I listened
to updates—the ongoing process of getting more Afghans out, the
State Department's efforts to process more special immigrant visas
and nail down commitments from more countries to accept Afghan
refugees—the weight of what was unfolding was evident. It was the
worst day of the Biden administration during my time there.

It was also the day of my daughter's kindergarten open house, which had been on the calendar for months. Vivi was incredibly excited about seeing her new classroom. I knew I needed to show up for her. When the meeting broke, I began calculating driving times in my head as I ran up to my office. I did not want to miss my daughter's big day and I knew that I could not let the president and the White House down. I needed help.

I checked my calendar: the open house was at 2:30 p.m. I asked Amanda, the chief of staff to the press office, to keep tabs on when the prep time would be scheduled for the president's remarks, and to print them out while I was gone, so I could review them in the short window I'd have before it was time to do my press briefing. I knew I would be cutting it close. The remarks review was scheduled for 4:00 p.m., which is when we would go through the president's remarks with him while he made edits. I needed to be back for that.

At 2:00 p.m., I slipped out of the White House, got in my car, and sped off to my daughter's elementary school in northern Virginia. I met Vivi and my husband in the parking lot, and we walked in hand in hand to see her classroom. My husband had seen the news that morning and assured me that if I couldn't make it, they would still have a great time and tell me all about it later. He also knew that I did not want to miss being there in person. I didn't have time to linger, but didn't want my daughter to feel rushed or to see that I was a little distracted. She pointed out everything in the room for inspection: the drawers full of art supplies, the cutouts of the sun and flowers on the walls, the small bathroom at the side of the room. We examined the book nook and her table. We met some of her classmates and their parents. We walked through the cafeteria and the gymnasium, trying out the basketball court, tricycles, and the playground.

I did my best not to look at my watch, but I caught glimpses of the time on the large clock on the library wall. It seemed to be ticking unusually loudly. Waves of emotion were washing over me—fear, sad-

ness, and anxiety, yes, but also gratitude. I had managed to be present
for my daughter in her big moment and fortunately she was ready to
go just around the time I really needed to make an exit. We hugged in
the parking lot and I rushed to my car.

By 4:00 p.m., I was flying down the hallway to my West Wing
office. I grabbed a binder with a draft of the president's remarks from
Amanda, who straightened the collar of my suit jacket just as the small
group of advisors walked into the Oval Office. The president really
wanted to get his statement right. He was always particular about his
remarks, but that remarks review was longer and more challenging than
normal.

The president didn't begin speaking until 5:24 p.m. In order to get
ahead of the evening news, I needed to directly follow him with the
briefing. This wasn't ideal. There wouldn't be time to type out my comments or to nail down small details. I would have to speak more from
my gut than from prepared points.

At 6:07 p.m., I began my daily briefing, and I was especially
straightforward. I talked about being in the room with the president
when he heard the news, his outrage over the attack, and his deep sadness over the loss. "Any day where you lose service members is—may
be—the worst day of your presidency," I said.

I spoke about the courage and commitment of the men and women
in the military and their sacrifice for their country. I explained why the
president stood by his decision to end the war. Then I opened it up to
the room. The press asked repeatedly about Americans being left on
the ground in Afghanistan, and I responded over and over that the
administration was working to extract every single citizen who wanted
to leave.

Forty minutes later, the press conference ended. When I returned
to my office, I took off my shoes and sat at my desk. The adrenaline

was wearing off, and it all caught up with me: the devastation of the tragedy, the intensity of the greater mission, and the weight on the shoulders of every member of the military.

I took a moment before bringing my team into my office. There wasn't a lot to say, but I thanked them for being by my side and for showing up on the hardest day so far, and especially for helping me manage my schedule when it seemed impossible at times. Then I hurried home to kiss Vivi and Matthew good night.

The first time I ever really asked for something big at a job, or a potential job, was when I was thirty-six years old. I was sitting in my living room one Saturday afternoon in 2015 when my phone buzzed. It was Denis McDonough, the White House chief of staff. At the time I was the spokesperson at the State Department, and my immediate worry was that Secretary Kerry must have said something that the White House was so mad about, it warranted a call from Denis. I braced myself when I answered.

But that wasn't why he was calling. He got straight to the point. "President Obama wants you to come back for the final stretch to be the communications director," he said. "I hope you'll consider it."

I loved working at the State Department, but when the president, or one of his representatives, calls and asks you to do something you just immediately say yes . . . right? For the first time, it wasn't that simple for me.

"I'm honored," I replied. "But I have to tell you something I haven't shared with many people yet—I'm pregnant and due in July."

After only fifteen seconds of consideration, I had talked myself out of the possibility of the communications director job, a role that oversaw the strategy and the messaging for the White House and the president. In that brief time span, I leaped to the conclusion that Denis would immediately decide that someone who was pregnant probably wasn't the right choice. I figured he would wish me good luck and move to the next name on his list. But that's not what he did.

"Congratulations," Denis replied. "I am so excited for you. We'll figure out how to make everything work for you. Just promise me you'll think about it."

"OK," I said. A bit stunned that the offer still stood in light of my personal news, I quickly realized that this was now a decision I would actually have to make myself. While I was a little daunted, I'm grateful that Denis didn't just accept my initial response and move on. When you let someone else make a decision for you, you're eliminating options you might actually want, and giving that person the power over your future. This can be appealing, because making decisions can be really difficult. But the fear of having to balance priorities, or make sacrifices, or deal with the consequence of your choice can limit your growth. Now it was up to me to decide: Did I want to return to the White House, and to one of the most demanding jobs in government, just months before having my first child?

President Obama called me the next day. I will always remember that he began by apologizing that he didn't have a lot of time because "the king" (of Jordan) was waiting outside his office. He told me that having children was the best thing that ever happened to him and would be for me as well. He assured me that the team would work with me to figure out everything I needed, if I were to take the job. Which, the suggestion was, I should.

My husband, Greg, and I sat down and talked about what would make the job possible. First, I needed twelve weeks of maternity leave. (At the time, there was no maternity leave policy in the federal government.) Second, we planned to put our daughter in daycare, and I wanted to be able to pick her up every day, which meant leaving work at 5:30 p.m. Greg would also need to arrive at his office a little bit later because he would be responsible for dropping her off in the mornings. I was a little nervous to ask but also confident in my requests when I proposed those terms. For the first time in my career, I felt like I had to prioritize my needs.

Luckily, there's not a lot of room for cinematic suspense here: Denis and President Obama agreed to my requests and even left the door open for me to ask for anything else I might need once I better understood the demands of being a new mom.

I was also a little worried about being judged by my colleagues and the wider world for choosing to work such a high-intensity job when I had a newborn. But my former colleague Bill Burton gave me a piece of advice that pushed me over the edge.

"You want to be able to tell your daughter that, when she was a baby, you did this job," he said. And when I was massaging my five-month-old's stomach while she screamed from constipation during a late-night prep call for a presidential prime-time address, I thought of Bill's advice. It will also make a great embarrassing story to tell when she's a teenager. And we will always have the photos of her playing on the floor with President Obama when I had to pick her up early from daycare and ended up staying for a few hours after the president's assistant begged me to bring her in to the Oval Office to lighten the mood on a tough day. That same afternoon, Denis took her outside to the playground on the South Lawn and even changed her diaper while I sat in on a meeting.

There were a handful of days that I couldn't manage to get away and Greg did the daycare pickup, but I did leave at 5:30 p.m. almost every night. I had been so worried to ask Denis for this accommodation, but it was far from the end of the world. People adapt. That's what cell phones and laptops are actually good for. My team got used to me leaving the office at 5:30 every day—and arriving around 7:30 a.m., which I was able to do because Greg took care of the morning duties. Gradually some meetings I needed to attend were scheduled earlier, and I started to receive the memos and documents I needed to review with enough time to do so in the afternoons.

That doesn't mean your team or your bosses will always adapt, but when something is important and you've established yourself as a key player, your managers may be more flexible than you expect. While people in their twenties today seem to be far more effective at setting boundaries at work, that is not true for everyone. It can be hard to make demands when you're just starting out—you haven't differentiated yourself from other potential employees yet. On the flip side, you may get to a point where you want to take a job, or be part of something new, but there are commitments in your life that require you to make certain asks first. For some of those asks, you have to be willing to walk away if your boss says no, which isn't always easy. If the White House had come back and said, "No, sorry—you have to stay until nine p.m. every day," I probably would have had to decline their offer. But I wasn't hired to be the communications director at the White House because they needed a warm body who was punching the clock. They wanted *me* to do the job, so they accommodated me as best they could. I did miss meetings. I did miss trips. And I couldn't work the same number of hours that I had before I was a mom. Those were choices I made.

It might have helped that I had never asked for special treatment, or said no to any request, before. I had effectively picked my battles for when I really needed to fight for something. But I can't claim any grand strategy on my part; I never asked for anything previously in my career because I'd been afraid of rocking the boat. I didn't realize you *could* ask for things while working at the White House, or even set reasonable limits. And the insanity of the way I worked before my daughter was born was frankly my own doing more than anything my bosses asked of me.

At the State Department, for example, I went on a trip lasting almost two weeks that included a stop in Afghanistan. I had a boot on my foot because I'd fractured multiple bones by basically ignoring the pain and continuing my running routine for so long that eventually I couldn't put pressure on the ball of my foot. Seriously—there was no accident, no dramatic fall. Just a refusal to slow down. It didn't occur to me to suggest that someone else go to Afghanistan in my place because of that injury. The boot allowed me to walk, after all. And it was a conversation starter. During a stop in Cairo, the foreign minister of Egypt even shared with me his experience of having a similar boot.

Less of a natural conversation starter on this trip: I had a temporary crown on one of my molars. This was not something I worried about; I'd had the temporary crown for months, and I'd forgotten it was there. The problem is, you're not supposed to forget about these; you're supposed to get them replaced with a permanent crown within a few weeks. I learned why when the entire thing fell out during a flight and I was left with the pointy, shaved-down remnants of what had been underneath. No, I did not go home, or seek emergency dental assistance; I put the crown in a little Ziploc baggie and carried it with me for the rest of the trip, hobbling through a war zone and several Middle Eastern countries with my boot on and half a fake tooth.

I wish I could say there was something gained by my being on this trip with broken bones and a missing tooth. But there wasn't. I'd known about both issues for weeks in advance; someone else could have easily taken the trip in my place. It wasn't that I wanted the glory or a professional opportunity that the trip provided; I just didn't feel like I could speak up (or take time out of the workday to go to the orthopedist or the dentist). I was afraid of missing out or showing any weakness. It was only once I had kids, and I had to make asks on not just my behalf but theirs, that I reached a point where I was able to establish some key boundaries.

I had always wanted kids, to be a mom, and as soon as this seemed like it might create tensions at work, I began asserting myself. By the time President Obama's second term was winding down, my confidence in speaking up about my needs as a working mother had grown. We were returning to the White House after a trip one day when President Obama asked how my daughter was doing in daycare. I told him we loved the women who took care of her there and we were grateful the center was nearby.

"There isn't a daycare at the White House?" he asked. Now, it may sound surprising that the president didn't know whether there was a daycare in the White House.* But let's not forget he was the leader of the free world during the worst financial crisis in a generation, the ending of the war in Iraq, and the passage of historic healthcare legislation, just to name a few of the things on his plate. And there weren't exactly dozens of women he interacted with every day in the White House who had daycare-age kids. His curiosity, and support for not only my maternity leave but also the maternity and paternity leave of several senior staffers during the final years of his presidency, actually changed precedent and expectations. The administration initiated both maternity and paternity leave policies while Obama was still in office, and a number of staffers took advantage of them in the last year and a half of his presidency. So, in the moment I was not surprised or disappointed that he didn't know if there was a daycare. He had once told me I was "normally an A student." The same was true of him.

"No," I replied, "and actually it would be so helpful in the future if there was a daycare on campus with flexible hours so parents could see their kids and also be able to stay later for meetings." For anyone wondering, there is still not a White House daycare.

By the time I went to work for President Biden, my personal circumstances had changed again: my daughter was now five and my son was two. I knew that I would need to set some parameters and carve out

---

* Decades earlier, First Lady Jacqueline Kennedy had started a daycare in the White House basement for about a dozen children, but there had not been any form of a daycare accessible to employees for many years.

my schedule to ensure I had quality time with them. During my interview for the press secretary job, he told me that if my kids ever had a doctor's appointment or a school event I should go, no questions asked.

I decided to try leaving "early" on Fridays, which meant at about 5:00 p.m. We had established a weekly pizza night with my sister and her family, and I wanted to be able to be there. Most of the time.

While I didn't exactly sneak out of the building, I also didn't announce I was leaving. At first, part of me felt guilty about going home before my colleagues did. But over time the people I worked closest with knew that barring an international crisis I would be leaving the office at 5:00 p.m. on Fridays. Sometimes I missed meetings; sometimes I left in the middle of something that wasn't critical. People accepted this. My decision to preserve this time for our family actually stemmed from a conversation I had with Rahm Emanuel about going back to work at the White House. His advice to me was that I needed to find ways to set boundaries, because the job was different with kids.

Rahm told me that when he was the White House chief of staff he would do his best to leave early on Friday nights to have Shabbat dinner with his family. One night, his phone rang in the middle of dinner. It was the president.

Rahm picked up and asked if it was an emergency, or if it could wait two hours. Of course it can wait two hours, Obama replied. That was it.

"Talent counts," the psychologist, researcher, and author of *Grit: The Power of Passion and Perseverance* Angela Duckworth tells her children. "But effort counts twice." When I was growing up, the rule in our house was that if you signed up for an activity, you had to finish it. You didn't have to continue forever, but you had to get to the end of the season, or that session of classes. It was a standard rule for previous generations of parents, and it makes sense: you want your children to develop a healthy distress tolerance, and I probably owe my willingness to try and try again—and yes, even to visit war zones with a boot on my foot and a missing tooth—to this toughness. My parents' rule has also helped me weather criticism that may be unfair or cruel (if somewhat valid) when I am not exactly excelling at something. But it also might have kept me from finding other things that I enjoy. I probably swam competitively way longer than I should have; I could have quit after or even during high school. I don't know what I would have done with the countless hours I spent in the pool, but maybe I would have started working in politics earlier, or actually learned to cook or paint or cross-country ski.

But sometimes quitting just is the right thing. You can do it badly or you can do it well. The latter is a better strategy. As Duckworth further writes, "Grit is not just about stubborn persistence. It's also about choosing the right goals." I have had a lot of jobs. Some of them ended because a campaign was over or the candidate I was working for lost. In those cases, I didn't need to give notice; we all just found ourselves unemployed. But there have also been a number of times when I've found myself with that nearly sick-to-my-stomach dread of telling a boss I was leaving.

Thanks to the long and stressful days like some I've described, White House jobs have a high turnover—they're draining, and people start to feel like they're too burnt-out to do their best work after a few years (or less). That means I've both quit and been quit on many times. It also means that it has been crucial to learn how to leave the door open for future opportunities. As my mom says, you don't have to burn down the building when you quit. There's a way to leave a job that preserves the very real possibility that you might want to work with your boss, or coworkers, again someday. Just as I have affection for everyone I've ever dated—seriously—I don't have any hard feelings about any job I've had, even the jobs I really didn't like (see my thoughts on consulting, below), and that freedom from resentment has given me the space to grow.

Working in the White House for President Obama the first time was a dream job. I respected him. I worked for people I looked up to and learned from and I had a literal front seat to history. But it was also an intense daily grind. I hit a point after the nearly two-year campaign and two and a half years in the White House where I was experiencing that burnout to such a high degree that I couldn't even enjoy my free time. I remember walking out of my apartment on a beautiful Saturday in May of 2011 and feeling so tired I just wanted to go back inside and crawl under my covers. That was a wake-up call.

It still took me a few months to quit. I wanted to give plenty of notice so had set a deadline for myself. When the day came and I couldn't put it off any longer, I was so worried about chickening out that I kind of sprung the news on my boss, Dan Pfeiffer. He was packing up for the day and I blurted out, "Hey, can I talk to you for a minute?"

It wasn't that I thought he was going to yell or shame me. I looked up to Dan. He was hardworking and smart and I had learned a ton by watching him. But I just couldn't do this job anymore.

He knew immediately. He was also about to leave for a well-deserved vacation. Great timing on my part.

"I know that you've thought about this a lot and that I am not going to convince you to change your mind, as much as I would like to. Can you just wait until I get back to tell anyone else?" It was a fair request. Whenever someone left the White House there was immediate speculation about why, and who would replace them.

So, I did wait. Once he was back from vacation, I scheduled meetings with a number of people in the building whom I wanted to tell directly. One by one I sat down with Valerie Jarrett and David Plouffe to let them know I had given notice.

I was sad about leaving the White House, and completely unsure about what was next for me. But it was still the right decision.

I have also quit jobs not because I was overwhelmed with exhaustion, but because I was getting a little too comfortable. When there's no more opportunity to grow, it's probably time to move on to the next challenge, no matter how great your boss or the schedule or the benefits are. That was my experience at the Carnegie Endowment for International Peace. I started working there in 2017, a little over eight months after Trump was elected. I didn't know it when I accepted the job, but I was pregnant with Matthew. Working at Carnegie was a great opportunity to gain a little more flexibility while working with smart, interesting people (who happened to leave at 5:00 p.m. and didn't work on Fridays in the summer).

I loved my time there—I built a team, I had a great boss in Bill Burns, and I definitely did not feel the weight of stress that comes with high-level government jobs. But after I hit the two-year mark, I knew I had to force myself to leave. I was starting to feel stagnant and a little bored with working at a think tank. I didn't quit because I had a bad boss or a bad work environment. Quite the contrary. I quit because I needed to keep pushing myself to take risks, to grow, and to do something different.

There have also been times I quit because the job wasn't the right fit. I have never been fired, but I'm well aware that I've been better at some jobs than others. I have worked for and with a number of consulting firms, and it's safe to say that consulting is not one of my superpowers. I don't love pitching business. I don't love advising companies or clients from the outside, only knowing a fraction of information about the challenge they are facing or what they are trying to achieve. I don't love offering advice and having it be ignored (a reality in any job, but it comes with the territory in consulting).

And still, a number of times between campaign and political stints,

I have found myself working as a consultant. I often liked the people I was working with and for, but I hated the work every single time, and always knew I was not as good in the role as the people who hired me thought I would be. It was a relief to quit those consulting gigs, knowing I was moving on to something else.

My point is we can't all be good at everything. Sometimes figuring out what you are terrible at is almost as valuable as figuring out your superpowers, because at least you can cross some options off the list of future endeavors. If a job requires consulting, singing, or bike riding I know I need not apply. And I am OK with that.

So, what's the right way to give notice? First things first: don't tell your work friends before you tell your boss, if you can help it. You never want your manager to hear you're leaving from someone other than you; it's unprofessional to not share your plans directly. When you're ready to give your notice—at least three weeks in advance, if possible—approach your direct manager and explain that you're ready to leave. (Unless you're in an industry where it's common practice to leave immediately—some media organizations do this to preserve journalistic integrity, for example.) This meeting is not about airing your grievances; it should remain cordial and straightforward, even if you hated the job with every fiber of your body. Of course, a lot of people leave jobs because they don't like them, whether because it's just not a good fit or because the company culture or the bosses themselves are toxic. If you think it would be helpful, you can set up a separate meeting, ideally with the HR department, to discuss these issues. You don't want to let your emotions get the better of you in this meeting—even if your manager is capricious, exploitative, and rude, they might be called for a reference someday, and there's no reason to hurt yourself because someone else doesn't know how to conduct themselves in the workplace.

As a manager, I want my employees to grow, and not to feel trapped or stifled in their jobs. The fact is, their growth trajectory may not have anything to do with me because there may not be another position to grow into on my team. When you receive a talented staffer's notice, you of course close your door and say, "*Shit!* She's so great! Now what will we do?!" But by being positive and generous, you have a chance of getting them back again someday, with all the new skills they'll collect in the interim. Rachel Maddow has some staffers who have worked with her for fifteen years. The rule on their team is if you leave you can always come back. The message is so powerful because it conveys: we support you growing and experiencing different things, but you also have a home here. The "roots and wings" philosophy of raising children also applies to managing. You want to make your employees feel connected to a solid foundation but also give them the confidence to fly.

9

Say Less

*On managing what you're not supposed to say
and keeping classified information to yourself*

I wanted to be able to say much more, publicly, about our efforts
to bring home journalist and political prisoner Jason Rezaian
(left). Somehow his wife Yeganeh (seen here with Jason and me)
didn't lose hope.

If you've ever watched one of my press briefings, or read the statements I gave to the press when I worked at the White House, you
might have gotten frustrated with me at times. Believe it or not, I get
it. It was my job to communicate, and occasionally, on certain topics,
I seemed to be saying far less than you would have liked to hear. "It's
an area we're looking into," I might have said. "The president is con-

cerned about this issue." "I am not going to be able to provide additional details right now."

While this kind of language can be infuriating to reporters and audiences who want straightforward answers and more information about what's happening in the world, limiting what you say publicly at times is part of the job description of any spokesperson, and particularly one who works in government. Discretion is of course valued in just about every industry, but when your job is to communicate, to be honest, and to help create an understanding of the inner workings of the government or other organization, your job is not actually to share everything you know about every internal debate or discussion. Doing so could preempt a decision that isn't final or put an important negotiation at risk.

There were many times, in both the White House and the State Department, that I knew a policy was going to change, or something was going to happen, but I couldn't say anything about it publicly. Experienced reporters know the stock phrases well. At the State Department, we had a number of responses we leaned into regularly. "That is an objective we have" signaled to reporters that they might be on to something, but I couldn't say more at the time. Sometimes I would repeat the reporter's question as a statement, or I would reiterate a very basic, well-known tenet of US foreign policy: "Preventing Iran from acquiring a nuclear weapon is certainly a goal of the United States." If all else failed, I'd go with the classic: "There's not more to provide right now."

Although this language may seem meaningless, it actually serves a very specific function. Experienced reporters also know that, although I may sound like I was saying nothing, I was importantly *not* saying things like, "No, we're not involved." Or, "No, we aren't considering that at all." Even broad or nondescript statements can effectively signal a position.

At times I actually had to fight to be allowed to provide even the most mundane statements. On a handful of particularly tricky days, other senior advisors to the president suggested I just not do a briefing. This happened during a tense moment in legislative negotiations around the infrastructure and Build Back Better bills. But my view was always that canceling a briefing also sent a message that maybe something was happening behind the scenes that we didn't want to talk about.

Even when you are limited in what you are able to say publicly, it's important to know the full scope of an issue or a debate. And that means being at the table.

This isn't always easy. You can't always just show up to any meeting you want. Oftentimes there are gatekeepers, and sometimes gatekeepers have good reasons for turning people away. But if you think having access to certain information will make you more effective at your job, whether through briefings, internal memos, or attendance at meetings, you should try to make the case for why you deserve a key to that gate.

I dealt with this at the White House. Many administrations debate over how much the press secretary should know about a range of policy discussions. Some press secretaries only wanted to know what they could share with the public; others liked to have more background information. How much access the spokespeople have is ultimately a collective decision within the administration.

Ron Klain, Biden's chief of staff, was definitely on the "need to know" side of the fence, and he had some compelling reasons. Based on many years of working with press secretaries as Biden's chief of staff when he was vice president, Ron thought I only needed to be aware of what I could talk about publicly. Knowing more, he reasoned, would put me in a difficult position that would require me to keep quiet about a lot of things I couldn't reveal, which even the most experienced spokespeople struggle with in high-intensity situations. I understood his argument. But I knew that I needed to attend certain meetings in order to effectively do my job, even if my job that day was to say very little. When I'd worked as the communications director, I'd been invited to sit in on national security and senior advisors meetings, which had given me a stronger foundation for my work.

Communications director is kind of like the city mayor, overseeing the big-picture public image of the administration, managing the majority of the communications staff, and developing strategic planning and messaging. The press secretary is the firewoman. As press secretary, I knew I'd be focused on day-to-day issues of being the spokesperson for the administration, and, yes, putting out fires. Still, my experience in the other role made me certain that if I wanted to do my best in this one, I needed to have the big-picture perspective that sitting in on these meetings would provide. Understanding the ins and outs of a debate or policymaking process would enable me to better translate the workings of government to the public.

I found that the less I knew about what was going on, the less I understood the reasoning behind a decision. Not knowing the difficult options that may have been discussed added time to my prep work of anticipating reporters' likely questions and how to answer them. If I knew the full picture, including specific details of decisions at every stage, I would be able to draft statements and respond to questions without hesitation, even if I had to massage the language or hold something back.

I've always operated according to a policy of picking my battles, and this was one battle I chose: I felt it was important for me to sit in on certain policy discussions. To his credit, Ron relented pretty quickly. And when it came to issues like the war in Ukraine, Jake Sullivan, who had spent years traveling with then–secretary of state Hillary Clinton and briefing the press as a small part of that role, understood instinctually why I needed to be in certain national security meetings to better articulate our policies.

The depth of my knowledge was especially helpful when communicating about controversial issues. That access wasn't unlimited—aside from the president, *everyone* has limitations on which meetings they attend—but when there was a big international issue, sitting in a room with the president, vice president, secretary of state, secretary of defense, director of national intelligence, chairman of the Joint Chiefs of Staff, and several other top-ranking officials made me better at my job. And when, after the meeting, I held a strong briefing that took responsible advantage of what I'd learned in the room, it further reinforced the wisdom of saving a seat for me, even if at times I was more of a fly on the wall.

As a spokesperson, I often had to act as the middle woman between my boss and the public. Sometimes that position is uncomfortable, and it requires saying less or nothing about your own personal view. It was hard, for example, in Obama's first term, to repeat his hesitation to support legalizing gay marriage. I had long been a supporter of gay marriage and LGBTQ rights, but that wasn't the stated position of the administration or the president until the spring of 2012 and it wasn't my place (or frankly the place of anyone else speaking on behalf of the president) to share my own views. For Biden, I often found myself as the spokesperson against the legalization of marijuana, despite the fact that I have long thought marijuana should be legal. Although Biden is the most progressive president in history on that issue, he's still not very progressive on it. But while I was White House press secretary, it wasn't my role to say what I thought; it was to explain the position of the president. So I would share that Biden supported the legalization of medicinal marijuana, decriminalization, and expanding research on the drug . . . even when I was asked about it on 4/20, which the not exactly left-wing Chuck Schumer referred to as the "unofficial American marijuana holiday" on the Senate floor while expressing his support to legalize the drug on the federal level.

Having to speak on behalf of a person you disagree with every now and then is not an unusual position to be in at work; if you're a lawyer, a manager, or a spokesperson, you'll inevitably have to argue on behalf of policies or people you may not be 100 percent aligned with. Hopefully that is rare and your values are generally shared by your employer. This may sound overly optimistic, but hear me out. I was never asked to lie or put anyone in danger, and I otherwise agreed with the administrations I was representing about 95 percent of the time. I decided that being a part of the greater good, of pushing progress forward, didn't require me to have 100 percent alignment. I just needed to believe that I was speaking on behalf of someone committed to making progress.

But this is another reason to advocate for being invited to meetings where big decisions are being made; if you establish yourself and your credibility, and pick your battles wisely, you may be able to effect change on the issues you believe in. Many of the meetings I attended concerned issues that were outside the purview of the press office, but I cared about those issues. In the Biden administration, several senior officials had young kids at home, so when discussing school closures during the pandemic, we were able to underscore the seriousness of the challenges, describe how frustrated other parents in our community were, and advocate for policies that we thought, from our experience, would best serve the American people. Many of us were mothers who sent our kids to public schools, so our real-life, first-person experience gave these meetings a perspective they wouldn't have had if only older white men were sitting at those tables.

I never shared classified information or put an administration's operations in jeopardy. But as you know by now, that's not to say I never misspoke or created more trouble for myself and the administration than I needed to.

I am human, and my temper can occasionally get the better of me; the PsakiBombs sometimes exploded. Toward the end of the Obama administration, Trump was getting more and more popular in the polls and I was becoming increasingly exhausted juggling the demands of new parenthood and the communications director job. During an interview with the *New York Times*, I was asked about the president's plans for campaigning for Hillary Clinton and I said this: "He has indicated he wants to spend a lot of time on the campaign trail, so when it's time to do that, we'll go out guns ablazing" (looking back I am not sure why the gun analogy was my first choice). I added, "We are actively thinking through how to use the president on the campaign trail—what works for the nominee, what works for him, and how to utilize his strengths and appeal."

The quote was incredibly milquetoast, but you may remember from the "Jen and Jay Show" when Obama was running for reelection that White House staff are bound in their communications by the Hatch Act, which regulates the separation between politics and government. The Hatch Act police love catching people in the wrong and calling them out publicly.

Technically, I wasn't supposed to say very much at all about Obama campaigning. In response to my quote, Obama's chief of staff, Denis McDonough, had a meeting at the White House counsel's office to discuss whether I'd violated the Hatch Act. No one told me about the meeting, and when I found out about it, this royally pissed me off. I didn't really take a beat to think about what course of action might be appropriate.

Instead, I busted into Denis's office, rushed past his assistant, and yelled, "Why are you having meetings behind my back? If you have a problem you can come talk to me!"

Before he could respond I stormed back out again, literally took a lap around the outside perimeter of the White House, and called my husband. "Well," I said, "I think I'm going to be fired today."

I didn't get fired, but I do regret losing my cool. I know it was in part due to fear that I may indeed have inadvertently violated the Hatch Act, and I did not want to receive a sternly written letter with my name on it. Regardless, I should have made an appointment to talk to Denis and explained my position calmly and reasonably. It wasn't necessary, or wise, to express my anger about not knowing about a meeting; a simple "I would have appreciated you including me in that discussion" would have sufficed. I'm fortunate that he didn't get too mad at me; I suspect it was because I picked my battles, and blew up so rarely, so in the moment I had earned a pass from Denis. And on that occasion I didn't actually receive a sternly written Hatch Act violation letter.

This was far from the only time I said more than I should have in a moment of frustration. In the middle of 2016, Fox News reporter James Rosen was working on a story about how, when I was at the State Department in 2014, portions of a video of a briefing about the Iran nuclear deal were deleted from the State Department website and the department's YouTube channel. A conspiracy theory quickly developed that I was trying to cover up something I'd overshared in the briefing.

The deleted segments—about eight minutes in total—included me suggesting that the talks between the United States and Iran had begun earlier than my predecessor had claimed. Although the transcript remained public and I had gone into much greater detail about the timeline at another briefing the same exact week, it emerged that someone in the State Department had ordered the editing of that video. The theory was that I'm the one who'd made that order. The State Department is a massive bureaucracy, and although I was there for two years, the truth is I have no earthly clue who edits videos. I certainly would not have made such an order, even if I knew who to ask.

This story was made worse by the fact that no one, not the State Department or anyone at the White House, defended me. That feeling of isolation put me on edge. So, despite the White House counsel's office telling me not to, I decided the only option was to defend myself.

This broke a pretty cardinal rule of communicating: when you are in the middle of a shitstorm, don't be your own spokesperson.

Most of the time, it was easy for me to sympathize with reporters, which helped me de-escalate situations. In any of my communications jobs, if a reporter called and yelled at me, which happened several times a week, it was almost always because they didn't get something—scoops, stories, attention in a press conference—and I understood their bosses were unhappy about it. Sometimes I could see they were only putting on a show for their boss's benefit, so they could say that they had given the White House a piece of their mind. Regardless, there was rarely any advantage to getting into a sparring match, so I'd wait for a moment to say something like "Are you done? OK. I'm hearing that you're frustrated because we didn't come to you for the interview." I would validate their frustration and then try to talk about the path forward so we could continue working together more productively. The closest I'd get to showing any emotion would be the slight edge in that question "Are you done?"

With the State Department video story, I could have accomplished my self-defensive maneuver with a single firm statement denying that I'd ordered the edit. But my frustration got the better of me when James Rosen, a reporter at Fox News, sent me a request for clarification on my original statement. On-camera he had been significantly less friendly, which I remembered as I pounded my response into a keyboard. "I understand it is inconvenient for you that I have nothing to do with this given you have spent the last three weeks vilifying me on television without any evidence of my knowledge or involvement and without once reaching out and asking me," I replied, "but I would encourage you to also ask the State Department if there is any evidence. A shred or any information at all that suggests I had any knowledge of this or any connection to this on any level. Hopefully you will find the time to spend on the range of global events happening in the world in between attacking my character.

"Consider that on the record from me as well," I added.

Well, that was a mistake. Of course, my email became its own story, and the White House counsel and State Department got pretty irritated with me, which resulted in a stern talking-to by the White House lawyers. Not unwarranted, to be fair. In retrospect, I certainly should have said less.

Good communication is sometimes about lowering, not raising, the volume. Just as an effective message doesn't need to be shouted, it also doesn't need to be long. If it is done carefully, fewer words can convey a much more powerful message. One of my favorite examples of this was embossed on my memory when I was a child. My parents almost never grounded me, and even when I did get in trouble my mother didn't yell. She was a lot like President Obama in this respect. She would simply say something like "I am so disappointed in you." That was a dagger—a clear message that what I had done was so bad, she didn't have the words to fully articulate her anger. In saying so little, she was saying so much. My youngest sister, Kristen, was all of fourteen years old when she was pulled over driving my parents' car, no particular destination in mind. My dad went to pick her up, and on the drive home he didn't say a word. I'm sure he was furious, but he knew that she had already experienced the necessary level of fear and embarrassment. At home, Kristen got the "I am so disappointed in you" from Mom. The delivery was so upsetting that Kristen grounded *herself* for a few months.

The less-is-more style can apply to public communications as well. My State Department briefing book contained etched-in-stone wording related to the Middle East, the South China Sea, and other regions. All had to be strictly adhered to—you did not want to color outside the lines. Reporters, the public, and even foreign governments might read into your slight change in wording, and when you're talking about parts of the world that are chronically on the brink of large-scale violence a single misplaced adjective might have drastic consequences. At the same time, a calculated change of a word or two might go over many people's heads but land a powerful punch elsewhere.

Less is more isn't always the right approach, but there are countless relationships that have enough context for a similar kind of shorthand diplomacy. Slight shifts in the way a chief financial officer delivers the report on the quarterly earnings call can send a message about the growth potential or projected losses of a company. A medical doctor from the Centers for Disease Control predicting an "uptick in COVID this fall" will certainly make my ears perk up. A coworker's stray remark over beers might be an alert that the boss is on the way out the door, or up the ladder. The key to a successful less-is-more strategy is knowing enough about your audience that you can narrow down, to the bare minimum, what they need to hear in order for them to receive your signal. That selectivity is what makes the strategy effective.

Throughout my time at the White House and State Department, I certainly knew much more about the president's and secretary's feelings about world affairs than I was allowed to say publicly, and I had no trouble communicating to reporters and the public in brief, concise language. But there were many times when my inability to say more was incredibly difficult. When you desperately want to tell someone what they want or deserve to hear, and you can't, it takes a lot of skill, and real conviction in your reason for holding back, to withstand the temptation to tell them everything you know.

Jason Rezaian's father immigrated to the United States from Iran in 1959. Jason was born and attended high school in Marin County,

California; he has both Iranian and US citizenship. After college, Jason became a freelance reporter based in Iran before being named Tehran bureau chief for the *Washington Post*. In 2014, Iranian security forces raided his apartment in Tehran, confiscated laptops, notes, and books, and arrested both Rezaian and his wife, the journalist Yeganeh Salehi. They were thrown into Evin Prison, a notoriously brutal detention center that houses political prisoners.

While Yeganeh was released on bail after three difficult months, Jason was denied bail and remained in prison. He was charged with espionage, an allegation frequently used by Iranian authorities to detain Westerners who report on the political conditions in the country. He was kept in solitary confinement. He suffered from several medical ailments, including a chronic eye infection that threatened his vision, and an agonizing inflammation in his groin. The psychological effects of his incarceration were also extremely painful. There wasn't evidence that he was getting adequate medical attention, and as a result it was entirely within the realm of possibility that he would die in Evin.

When American citizens are detained by authoritarian regimes, getting people out involves sensitive negotiations that could be jeopardized if they are made public. The most effective way to extract Americans from countries where they're detained illegally is to do it quietly, only announcing the release when the prisoner is on a flight back to the United States. Yeganeh was one of the only visitors allowed to see her husband in prison, and she tirelessly advocated for his release, keeping Jason's situation on the media's radar. As State Department spokesperson, I was asked several times a week, for months, about Jason's status.

"What is the administration doing to bring him home?" was the obvious and correct question, and my dissatisfying answer was always the same. "We are monitoring the situation closely," I would say, or, "We are doing everything possible to bring Jason home."

I imagined being in Yeganeh's position, and thought that I would have hated the line "we are doing everything possible." Who is "we," what is "possible," and how do you define "everything"? We don't want a full inventory of the 150,000 things going on in their lives when we ask a friend, "How's everything?" If someone says, "I did everything possible to get that dog to stop barking," they almost certainly didn't do *everything*, if for no other reason that there are laws against doing some of those untried things. If you were following Jason's detainment, when you heard me say something like "We are doing everything possible" you might think it was nothing but hot air. Politicians make a lot of promises about what they'll do, and how hard they're working to get these things done, but upon closer inspection that "everything" is often revealed to be "a few things, executed halfheartedly, maybe."

Of course, there was a lot more to the story. At the time, you may remember, the United States was part of an international group trying to negotiate a deal with the Iranian government to better contain their nuclear weapons. Human rights activists insisted that Jason's detainment be a part of that discussion. The editor of the *Washington Post* even called for the US to think twice about proceeding with the negotiations over a nuclear deal unless the country would discuss Jason's release.

So, silence it was. There were some days when I walked out of the briefing room thinking, *If we can't talk about what we're doing to try to get an innocent journalist out of prison, how will his family and loved ones and supporters have any hope?* Hearing the same stock phrases, briefing after briefing, how could Yeganeh keep faith that the administration's commitment wasn't just lip service? It was impossible not to imagine Yeganeh—who was not privy to every detail of what was going on behind the scenes, given how sensitive and classified the efforts were— being anything but bitter.

But Yeganeh was just one of several audiences I was speaking to—I was also addressing members of Congress and the military, our allies, the Iranians, and the American public. All of them heard the same phrase. I needed them to hear it in the right way, depending on what their "right way" was, and the more elaboration I offered, the higher the chance of distracting from the mission and inspiring politicized criticism. I was among the small group in the White House who were aware that the negotiations to bring Jason home were in the final stages, so I knew much more than I could tell. That's why it was so maddening. All I could do was hope that he'd be freed and home so that I could finally show some emotion when I mentioned him in a press conference.

And then, after 544 days in prison, Jason was released as part of a prisoner swap on the same cold January day that the nuclear deal began implementation. By that time, I had moved from State to the White House to serve as President Obama's communications director. I still felt deeply connected to the story, and once I received the internal alert over email that Jason was in safe airspace, I exhaled a huge sigh of relief.

Two months later, my desk phone in the West Wing rang. It was my old friend Ben Rhodes, now a deputy national security advisor, asking if I could pop over to the EEOB (Eisenhower Executive Office Building) across the street for a quick meeting, subject unsaid. It was late afternoon, and I was pretty worn down. There were a lot of magic days in my job, but also some where I just wanted to get home to my infant daughter. This was one of those days.

Just steps away from the West Wing, the EEOB is enormous. The ornate ceilings and intricate tiles that line the hallways are much more impressive than the décor in a lot of the West Wing, which is much smaller than you realize before you spend nearly every day for several years there. As I walked into one of the grand rooms, I spotted a familiar face: it was Jason Rezaian, sitting next to Yeganeh! I was thrilled to see them together, looking so happy and healthy.

Yeganeh rushed over and gave me a huge hug.

"Thank you," she said. "On the days where I did not think there was hope, I would hear you say, 'We are doing everything we can to bring Jason home,' and that gave me comfort."

I felt unworthy of her praise and remembered how frustrating it had been to deliver the same narrow and limited response over and over. Now I knew that for Yeganeh, it was enough.

It was an important lesson. Words—spoken and unspoken—can emotionally connect strangers even when they seem bland in the specifics or vague in their promises. The same sentence that was annoying to many reporters in its obscurity was uplifting to another. Despite my anguish at not being able to give Yeganeh the support, hope, and comfort I felt she deserved, I had managed to do just that.

But there was something else, too. For Yeganeh the "less" was "more" because of context. If I hadn't built up a substantial degree of credibility, and wasn't working for a boss with the same, it would have been much easier to doubt that what I was saying had any basis in fact. That credibility bolstered my message.

As I watched those two courageous journalists chatting joyfully, the day after Jason's fortieth birthday, I was grateful to be in their company. And then I went home to explain to Greg why I was so late. "I did everything possible to bring myself home sooner," I explained, "but I was monitoring the situation closely, and I needed to see how it would end." He rolled his eyes and then laughed at my exhausted attempt at humor.

10

Russia Says You're Getting Fired?

*On dealing with rumors, gossip, and bullying,
from Vladimir Putin or your office frenemy*

Sometimes the president tunes in to the White House briefing (and often has questions of his own afterward).

REPORTER: *A lot of Americans are saying that, you know, the surges are happening under President Biden's watch after he reversed some previous policy. So does the administration take any accountability for what's happening?*

ME: *Who are the Americans?*

REPORTER: *Well, I know you don't want to answer to him, but the former president just released a statement saying that "the Biden administration must act immediately to end the border nightmare that they have unleashed onto our nation."*

ME: *Former president Trump?*

REPORTER: *Yes.*

ME: *We don't take our advice or counsel from former president Trump on immigration policy, which was not only inhumane but ineffective over the last four years. We're going to chart our own path forward, and that includes treating children with humanity and respect, and ensuring they're safe when they cross our borders.*

One of Donald Trump's favorite media strategies is to refer to non-specified "people" who just happen to be "saying" exactly the same thing he's been saying. If you don't hear the sarcasm in there about how I feel about this tactic, read again.

Part of the issue is of course that Trump has a relationship with the truth that is generously described as tenuous. He loves to quote straw men, nameless groups of made-up "people," because he knows those arguments can be effective. Of course, there are likely some "people," somewhere, who agree with him, and would "say" so. But "people are saying" implies a collective group that directly challenges an opponent (in this case, President Biden, or me).

Trump isn't the only public person who relied on the straw-man approach, and it isn't entirely new. But it has definitely increased in the years since he has been in the political spotlight. The White House reporters who covered Trump encountered this move so often that some of them began to adopt it themselves; after all, these were the same tactics that were used *against* the media throughout Trump's presidency, so reporters know how effective they can be. During my time as press secretary, I was asked many questions based on the premise that "some are saying" or "many people are saying."

I usually responded with a question. When a reporter would start off with something like "Critics are saying that President Biden is underestimating how hard it is to get a bipartisan bill passed . . ." my response would be fairly journalistic in turn: Who are those critics? Are they a few people the reporter surveyed on the street? Are they people who worked in politics twenty years ago? Are they current members of the Senate? Is it your neighbor?

Anonymous critics shouldn't put you on the defensive. Isn't there a big difference in how much you value the opinion of a random stranger versus a leader in your industry? Of course every voice matters, but some have a more direct impact on the outcome than others. And the question of which group can have the greatest impact depends on the situation. If we're talking about people complaining about the president's legislative strategy, a nebulous group of "critics" is very different from a small group of senators. The former might represent the majority or a tiny minority; they might have little information on whatever they're being asked about, or they might have preexisting biases that are relevant. Or they might be people in a small-town diner who were interviewed by a reporter. Those voices are important, but it wouldn't be accurate to say they represent the majority of people, or that their point of view would have an immediate effect on the president's policies. By contrast, if a group of senators was questioning the president's ability to enact policies he was pushing, their perspective would mean something different.

When I am interviewing people on my MSNBC show, I have undoubtedly slipped into this phrasing at times. It can be awkward and uncomfortable to ask critical questions. Framing tough questions with a passive "some have said" can help the questioner, or interviewer, avoid having to put forth her own view, which can also be useful when you're dealing with subjects who may be combative or strongly disagree with you. But I try to catch myself and instead quote a specific person and what she brought to the issue. Readers, viewers, and listeners need to know that context. And as I demonstrated in the back-and-forth I had with the reporter about immigration policy, if the "Americans" who are "saying" something can be boiled down to Donald Trump himself, it would only be worth commenting on if he *didn't* criticize something Biden was doing.

But as the events of January 6, 2021, demonstrated, Trump's spreading of rumors and conspiracy theories led to serious and horrific consequences. At 1:42 a.m. on December 19, then-president Donald Trump tweeted that it was "statistically impossible to have lost the 2020 Election." He went on to say there was going to be a "Big protest in D.C. on January 6th" and encouraged people to "Be there, will be wild." His acolytes interpreted this as a call to arms. Many of the hundreds of people arrested that day referenced how Trump's tweet motivated them to travel to Washington, some gathering weapons along the way. His words to his millions of followers on Twitter sparked a group of insurrectionists to storm the Capitol building for the first time in history. And his threats against law enforcement, district attorneys, prosecutors, and other politicians have unquestionably led to a rapid increase in threats and violence against public servants. His words had devastating consequences for the people still reeling from the trauma of that day.

Rumors and disinformation rarely spread because of positive intentions. Unlike the occasional "white lie" that's intended to avoid hurt feelings, disinformation can take a variety of forms in our personal and professional lives. Call it gossip, the rumor mill, conspiracy theories, or just plain lies: a company that engages in a multi-billion-dollar lobbying campaign encouraging teenagers to vape and the kid who slipped mean notes about you into your friends' backpacks during seventh-grade math class have more in common than the magnitude of their offenses might suggest. The good news is that some of the strategies you might use with the jerk from seventh-grade math class can still be applied to much bigger bullies.

While conspiracy theorists have probably existed since the first caveman returned to his cave to find his favorite club mysteriously, inexplicably missing, nothing in human history has done more to turbocharge the spread of disinformation than the pairing of celebrity culture and the growing reliance on social media platforms for information. Those algorithms do not reward facts and measured statements. Instead, clickbait headlines, salaciously worded posts, and personal attacks drive the most traffic. Old-school gossip columns were certainly catty and speculative, but the opportunity to publish instantly and without oversight means the online ecosystem opens up more potential spaces for rumors to spread much faster. And if it's hard enough to engage over matters of actual substance, it can be that much harder to address the unsubstantiated claims and narratives appearing in front of you as fast as your harshest critic can press "send."

This spreading of disinformation is not just about pop stars and actors. Over the last twenty years, nearly every public person, from influencers to politicians, has been run through the social media machine. My online critics have ranged from calling me a communist, to posting vomit emojis in response to statements I've made or things I have worn, to even sending personal threats. I've even gotten texts from people who found my home address and the names of my children. Not funny. But the occasional comment has almost made me laugh. For example, when I was still appearing as a political contributor on CNN at nearly nine months pregnant, someone suggested I had "let myself go." Thanks, sir! I was actually just carting around an almost fully cooked baby.

Some of the rumors and conspiracy theories around me have been relatively low-stakes, and even kind of funny—like the time in 2021 when Jill Biden wore an Oscar de la Renta dress with a lemon print on it to give a speech at an awards ceremony and the tabloids spent weeks trying to determine what covert message the First Lady had intended with the dress. Why? Meghan Markle had worn the same one weeks before.

When it was revealed much later in a British tabloid that Meghan sent a box of lemons to Dr. Biden as a nod to the dresses, another brief round of conspiracies arose. How did the lemons get there? Who delivered them? This I can clear up once and for all. It was me! I delivered the lemons. Meghan asked a mutual friend for help sending lemons to the White House. They were sent to my house instead (because it would have taken weeks for the lemons to make it through security, which would have resulted in a box of rotting lemons being delivered from the duchess to the First Lady; now that would have sent a different message). Some conspiracies are just silly when you know the facts.

Other times, though, being the target of disinformation did get under my skin—to the point that I dread the response from certain corners of the internet if I write about it here. But one thing I have learned from years under a bit of public scrutiny is that for the most part, just as you shouldn't put too much stock into the positive feedback you receive on the internet from people you don't know and who definitely don't know you, you also shouldn't put much weight on the negative feedback. The good comes with the bad. And haters are going to hate, especially online.

The lessons I learned in dealing with some of the most aggressive—if not the most subtle—propagandists in the world might help anyone who finds themselves up against a nasty rumor.

In 2014, when Russia invaded the Crimean Peninsula in Ukraine, I was the State Department's spokesperson, responsible for articulating our opposition to the invasion five days a week in my daily briefings. I did not hold back. I called the invasion illegal. I called President Putin a pariah. I said Russia was attempting to cover up the fact that they were sending young men to die in Ukraine for a war their par-

ents didn't know they were fighting. These were the positions of the
president and the State Department and I was on board. I defended
the Obama administration's decision to impose visa bans and sanctions
against Russia for the country's brutal annexation of the region. Every
single day we made clear that the actions of the Russian government
were illegal and immoral, as well as further isolating President Putin
and Russia from the rest of the world. It turns out the Kremlin didn't
like that very much.

Although I was not determining the policy of the United States,
my name, comments, and even sometimes my picture were included
in much of the coverage of Russia that followed each briefing. Among
those paying attention to my comments was Dmitry Kiselyov, a Russian TV presenter and propagandist. Kiselyov was a man of strong
opinions; he once compared Putin to Joseph Stalin, in a good way.
He was less favorable toward me. And he was one of the more public
ringleaders of a propaganda effort against Western officials. He coined
the term "psakiing," which he defined as making "a dogmatic statement
about something they don't understand, mixes the facts up, and then
doesn't apologize."

If you've never been turned into a verb by a Russian propagandist
and are wondering how it feels, I can tell you: not great! I knew intellectually that being attacked by Russia had little to do with my actual
performance. But the campaign, conducted by several Putin-friendly
media outlets, with the support of Russian authorities and their social
media foot soldiers, was relentless, constantly questioning whether I
was up to the job. And whether they knew it or not, I felt vulnerable to
that question. I was on a huge stage during a moment of historic, horrific conflict and wanted to get everything right.

But despite all my research and prep, I occasionally made mistakes.
Soon Russia Today, or RT, the state-run news channel that spewed
Kremlin talking points across the globe, started dedicating a nightly

news program to criticizing me, complete with slideshows of my biggest "gaffes." Their favorite example, which they ran over and over, stemmed from a briefing in early April 2014 when I incorrectly stated that natural gas largely flowed from Europe to Ukraine and Russia instead of the other way around. I immediately corrected myself—I had just misspoken, not misunderstood—but RT and other propaganda outlets seized the original comment sans correction to insist that I was ill-informed. No wonder Russian bloggers frequently reported I was being fired. (I wasn't.)

But what made their attacks so upsetting—frustrating, maddening, distracting—was that it wasn't usually an actual mistake they were harping on, but things I'd never done. RT aired daily segments featuring quotes I never said. They sent "reporters" to my briefings nearly every day to dramatically hold up bogus newspaper clippings and demand a response. Dmitry Rogozin, the former ambassador to NATO who was then a deputy prime minister, tweeted that my briefings lacked a "laugh track" and suggested to Foreign Minister Sergey Lavrov that he bring me some textbooks. Even when they quoted "accurately," they presented those comments out of context in ways that made it look like I was attempting to dodge the truth. There were stories of a warrant for my arrest in Crimea. Reporters who were doing stints in Russia would send me photos of my distorted face on T-shirts, and I heard a rumor that someone had seen my face on a deck of playing cards with the phrase "Enemy of the State" on them. I never did find those playing cards. If you have a pack, I would love to keep them for my future grandchildren.

Some of the most knowledgeable national security reporters thought it was funny, but at the time I wasn't so sure. Being attacked and having disinformation spread about you can feel isolating, no matter the source. I worried for my safety to a certain degree, but I was more worried that all this negative attention would reflect poorly on me: maybe people I worked with, from reporters to White House staff, would start to believe some of it. The stories were so relentless that I worried they had the power to plant doubt in my audience's mind about my credibility. Maybe my colleagues would come to think of me as a liability simply for the fact that I was such a known target. And of course being under so much pressure made me more likely to actually make a serious mistake, which I definitely did not want to do in such a volatile situation.

I couldn't exactly complain about my plight to John Kerry, my boss, who was trying to negotiate peace in the Middle East, end the war in Ukraine, and keep the nuclear deal with Iran on track. Plus, I was wary of looking weak or shaken to my State Department colleagues. As you may recall, I didn't have a lot of direct experience in foreign policy when I took the job, and I felt I needed to prove my value. Many of my colleagues had served in war zones. And in the grand scheme of things, being relentlessly mocked by a world power didn't compare to the suffering the victims of Putin's regime were experiencing, and continue to experience.

But the attacks did get in my head. During a long van ride with about a half-dozen members of Kerry's team through the winding roads of rural France in the summer of 2014, I was busy checking the one hundred–plus messages that had accumulated while I had spent the day dealing with a broad range of inquiries from reporters. While scrolling through, I stopped on a question from a TV reporter about Russian criticism of my performance. This was not one of those vague remarks like "some people are saying your performance at the State Department reveals a lack of experience." It was very clear who the critics were; I couldn't escape them. The reporter implied the attacks had negatively affected diplomacy between the two countries. What was my response?

I sat silently and tried to think, but I just wanted to take a nap.

When we stopped to pick up snacks and sandwiches for the rest of the ride, I caught up with some of the reporters who were traveling with us, including the former Moscow bureau chief for a major newspaper.

"Hey," he said. "Is something wrong?"

At first, I was embarrassed that he had noticed I was distracted and down, but then it all spilled out. I explained that the Russian propaganda campaign was making me feel awful. It was terrible to have my credibility attacked over and over, to the point that US reporters were expecting me to defend myself against these outrageous lies. I didn't know what to do: If I did respond to their questions, wouldn't I be perpetuating a false story? Even worse, I'd be placing myself at the center of that false story. Part of the point of the propaganda campaign, I knew, was to distract from the war, so any comment from me would, in some small way, help Russia in that goal. What a mess.

Without hesitating, he said, "You should know that the Russians trying to discredit you is a badge of honor. They did this to Secretary Clinton. They did this to Ambassador Mike McFaul and they do it to anyone who they worry will break through to their public."

He wasn't advising me what to do or not do. That wouldn't be the role of a reporter and certainly was never going to be a line this particular reporter crossed. But he could put into perspective something a lot of people, including members of the media who didn't have as much experience with the Kremlin, were missing.

As I climbed back into the van clutching my turkey and cheese sandwich, I felt a weight lifted. I still had to figure out the best way to deal with the TV reporter's inquiry, but my view on the Russian personal attacks had changed. If the Russians were bothered enough to criticize my character and what I wore, and to host an entire evening show about me, then maybe I was doing something right. The message of the United States was breaking through.

In early June, I decided it was time to push back. I prepared a response, which I rehearsed and workshopped with Ben Rhodes. I was more nervous than usual as I stepped up to the podium. (Funny how that works—the more important it is that you keep your cool, the harder it is to do it.) It didn't take long for a member of the press to broach the subject.

"So just a quick look at Twitter feeds over the last week—looks like in defending US policy from criticism, you yourself have come under criticism in some interesting language and ways," said Lara Jakes, an experienced foreign affairs journalist with the Associated Press. "I'm just wondering if you have any indication if these—this criticism, these tweets—are from official sources, or just freaks out there, I guess."

The pressroom laughed. Her tone wasn't combative—in calling my critics possible "freaks," Jakes made it easy for me to launch in.

"Well, I appreciate the question," I said. "I will say I'm in good company, because I'm just one of many American officials, especially women, targeted by the Russian propaganda machine. They do seem to have a bit of a tendency to focus on the outfits I'm wearing."

This was true: the Russians did target women more frequently than men, and their critical commentary often fixated on what those women were wearing. It was also a smart thing to bring up, because it framed the Russian attacks as frivolous, misogynistic, and immature. Indeed, they weren't to be taken seriously, but laughed at.[*]

"And so," I continued, "you'll have to ask them whether that's how great powers should make their case on the world stage. I think it's a pretty clear sign that they don't have the truth on their side. . . . So, if I get dinged a bit for that, I'm not going to sweat it. I will take it as a badge of honor."

In the briefing that day I wanted to do more than reframe the

---

[*] Years later, Putin brought up my name unprompted in a press conference in the days surrounding a meeting he had with President Biden. He described me as a "young, educated, and pretty woman," who was also "mixing things up all the time."

criticism of me as part of a general pattern; I also wanted to make it clear that the Russian propaganda attacks were not just trivial and sexist, but part of a more deceitful, and serious, attempt to "blame the messenger." As I explained, "stating plainly that Russia has had a hand in the unrest in eastern Ukraine is not, quote, 'uninformed,' as they suggest. It is stating the facts. Second, calling on Russia to pull back troops and engage directly with the government of Ukraine is not, quote, 'confused,' as they suggested. It is the position of the United States government, the G7 countries, and most of the world." By calling out *why* they were attacking me and staying focused on what I wanted to communicate about the illegality of the Russian invasion into Ukraine, I reframed the discussion to my advantage.

It was, as always, a question of audience. Putin was not my audience, and I was not responding directly to Russia's personal abuse; I was addressing it in a way that allowed me to take control of the narrative. Of course, most of the reporters I was speaking to knew that the Russian stories were bogus. But by showing I was being attacked for simply doing my job, which was articulating the position of the United States about Russia's illegal invasion of Ukraine, I was exposing their motivation for attempting to discredit me. Russia's attempts to slander me weren't only wrong but made them look weak and a little desperate. It wasn't a smoked-salmon joke (though they do love smoked fish in Russia), but it was part of my effort to expose the motivation for their attacks, making them less effective.

Humor can be a great tool for brushing off unfounded criticism. When I fractured the bones in my foot, for example, I had to wear a walking boot for eight weeks. This was already a bit comical, just to see it, but somehow even this set off the Russian propaganda machine, which transformed the situation into one that was truly absurd. One conspiracy suggested that the boot on my foot was somehow impacting my ability to answer questions about Ukraine. Another questioned where my other boot was, as if orthopedic boots were only worn in pairs.

I didn't want to spend any extra energy on the boot conspiracies; it was exhausting enough walking around in a boot. So I just dismissed these stories with a pun: "That's a new form of creativity in terms of their efforts to misconstrue the facts on the ground."

In the end, one of the best ways to combat disinformation is to mine the inevitable gaps between fact and fantasy. Here, again, is an audience question. Imagine for a second that the walking-boot conspiracy was becoming a true distraction. I could talk about it in a press conference, but it's a safe bet that just about everyone in the room would have known the whole thing was ridiculous, and they might have wondered why I was devoting time to it when so many more important things were going on. Or I could get out my phone and make one of those "What's in my bag?" YouTube videos, call it "What's in my boot?," and turn the entire thing into a parody as I extracted microphones, laptops, a telescope, fake eyeglasses, a trench coat, and a Russian cookbook from my orthopedic boot. The boot conspiracy was already mockable, but by turning it into a true joke I could take even more power away from the conspiracy pushers. Believe me, I thought about it, but I decided to take the high road.

A few years later, when I was back in the White House working for President Biden, Russia again invaded Ukraine. This military campaign was larger and more aggressive. It has displaced hundreds of thousands of people, destroyed historic cities and towns, and left a country reeling. As devastating as the war has been, the US government learned a lot about how to combat Putin's propaganda from what didn't work back in 2014 and 2015. Many of the same people, from national security advisor Jake Sullivan to director of national intelligence Avril Haines to director of the Central Intelligence Agency Bill Burns and Secretary of State Tony

Blinken, were in positions of power in the Biden administration, and they worked to declassify information about Putin's plans, to call him and the Kremlin out on their lies, and even to show the progress of the Ukrainian military. That proactive approach to fighting back helped rally the world, including the American public, around Ukraine.

Sometimes locating even a trivial contradiction between fib and reality is enough to give you an opening. In the weeks after the invasion of Ukraine in 2022, the United States sanctioned President Putin. In response, the Russians sanctioned Joseph Robinette Biden. As press secretary, I was asked if this was a significant escalation. Instead of condemning the sanctioning, I decided to point out that the Russians had made a gaffe, telling the assembled reporters, "I would first note that President Biden is a Junior, so they may have sanctioned his dad, may he rest in peace." The laugh that followed didn't mean reporters would stop asking the question about whether we thought the escalation was significant. But maybe they would think for a moment about how incompetent the Russians were. And it's always nice to land a zinger.

My work bully was Vladimir Putin, but yours might just be down the hall. If a colleague is spreading rumors about you, there are two basic ways to handle the situation. The first is to confront them directly. I didn't "go direct" to Vladimir Putin because I had no hope of changing his opinion of me (and I probably couldn't have spoken to him directly even if I'd wanted to). But if there's a chance of getting your message through, a calm, straightforward confrontation can be the best approach. I am not suggesting you storm into an office or send a harshly worded email. Instead, write up what you want to say to clarify your thoughts, practice it out loud if you need to (in front of your mirror at home or even your dog), and then ask to see the person causing the problem.

As with any difficult conversation, you should be direct and to the point, but stay calm. If you heard a coworker is spreading a rumor that you're lazy and your work is shoddy, the conversation could go something like this: "I hope I'm wrong, but I've heard that you have some concerns about my work product and work ethic. If you have these concerns you can come to me directly in the future." This may sound like giving in and agreeing to what this person might be criticizing you for, but you're not actually trying to have a conversation with them about your work—if they're not your boss, why should you talk to them about your performance? The aim of this conversation is to let them know you're on to them, and to ask them to stop spreading rumors.

If the rumor has spread through the team, you may need to make a broad statement about its accuracy. Let's say the rumor—that you are leaving for another job at another company—is completely false. In this case, you could ask your direct supervisor if you can say something at the end of a team meeting and then keep it simple: "I just wanted to nip something in the bud, because I've heard some chatter that you all think I am leaving for another job. I just wanted to clear up that I am not, and if anyone has any concerns, or hears anything about my plans from someone who is not me, I hope you will come speak to me directly."

If the rumor is *true*, you might have to come up with a new plan. If you really are leaving the company, you may have to disclose that to your manager sooner than you'd planned; otherwise, the story could snowball, and result in some hard feelings around your departure.

Sometimes people hear gossip that makes them scared and nervous, and if you're a manager in that situation, you may have to make a difficult decision about how to proceed. If there are rumors your company is being purchased, it's natural that employees would worry about what that might mean for their jobs. Sometimes all you can do is recite a vague placeholder statement: "I know there have been a number of rumors about the future of our company and that can be hard to hear and distracting. There's not more information at this time. As soon as there is I will share it with you. But in the meantime, the best thing we can all do is focus on the work we are producing." Acknowledging the existence of rumors and having these conversations out in the open will help your team feel like you're all on the same page. Ideally, you would share enough information so that people have what they need to do their jobs, without being distracted by the allure of speculating about secrets.

All that said, a certain amount of office gossip is unavoidable. Though you should aim to stay above the fray, and you definitely don't want to cultivate a reputation as someone who's always in the middle of the juiciest office drama, it's not realistic to expect someone to completely abstain from talking about the crazy thing that just happened in the hallway. We're all human. Gossip isn't just a vehicle for news and reputation; it's also a way of connecting with others and understanding the social dynamics of the environment you're in, which can be especially important in high-stakes industries. Especially if you're in a senior position, the office can be lonely. There are few people with whom it's appropriate for you to discuss off-the-record rumors and speculations and even frustrations, and you may know significantly more or significantly less about an issue than the average employee. That's why finding and forming a "trust squad" is essential to executing any job, and for protecting your own sanity.

Your trust squad is made up of the coworkers who cheer for you publicly and root for you behind the scenes, who let you vent without judgment and give you advice, including when you screw something up, and who know what you're struggling with and can make you laugh on good days and bad. Having these kinds of supportive colleagues also allows you to compartmentalize frustrations, stresses, and challenges so they don't dominate your thinking—you have a safe place to dump them. That means instead of blowing up at someone on your team you can get your irritation out of your system by venting to the trust squad first, then addressing the issue more calmly with your team member. It also means you don't constantly unload your work frustrations on your spouse, or bore your friends when you are out to dinner with them. You might also turn to your trust squad for advice in your personal life, whether it is about a sick parent or difficult child or even just the trouble you're having sleeping or balancing work and the rest of your life. Whenever possible, surround yourself with these people. They are rare.

Dana Remus was a key member of my White House trust squad. A brilliant lawyer, Dana served as the deputy White House counsel in the Obama administration and then as the White House counsel during the Biden administration. Dana had a huge job that required both an encyclopedic knowledge of past US law and the creativity to mold it for the future. Traditionally, there's a bit of friction between the communications and legal teams in the West Wing. This makes sense when you consider their goals. A communications person aims to make information understandable to everyone, while a lawyer aims to make information understandable to a smaller audience including other lawyers and sometimes a jury; in pursuing that aim, the communications person might elide certain small, but legally important, details that don't register to a general audience. Dana and I didn't always agree, but our connection wasn't about that. When we felt frustrated because we were excluded from a meeting or because a colleague was dismissive, we would talk to each other. Whenever we closed the door to my office for a debrief, people assumed we were discussing a tricky legal issue and left us alone. Sometimes we were, but sometimes we were just discussing how to navigate tricky dynamics in the office or even the balance with having a family.

Another member of my longtime professional trust squad is Katie McCormick Lelyveld, whom I met when we were in our mid-twenties sitting on the floor of the Kerry campaign office in Iowa the night he won the caucus. It was our task to sort through which reporters would fly with us to New Hampshire. Everyone wanted a seat on that plane. It had been a long day and it was just the start of a long campaign. Still, Katie and I didn't stop laughing as we worked through the night, sitting on the dirty floor. We worked together again early in the 2008 Obama campaign, betting on a long-shot candidate who many believed wouldn't make it through the primary process. When we both ended up with White House jobs—Katie became the press secretary to First Lady Michelle Obama, and I became a deputy press secretary working for Robert Gibbs—my office was in the West Wing and hers was in the East Wing, so we would meet in the Palm Room, halfway between, to gossip, vent, or just have a moment of easy conversation before getting back to our breakneck daily routines. We talked about opportunities we hoped to have in our jobs and promotions we were working toward. We also talked about our families, our boyfriends at the time, and how difficult it was to explain the stress and the responsibility on our shoulders to our college friends.

I've had work wives and husbands, like Jennifer Davis with whom I traveled the world while I worked at the State Department. Or Ben Rhodes, who time and time again was my hype man and booster, even when I was being pummeled by actual authoritarian dictators.

Working at the White House is similar to working in many stressful environments. Not everyone is entirely trustworthy, even if you enjoy working with them. In a competitive environment, it's unfortunately true that some coworkers try to use rumors and gossip to their advantage. Having people you trust with whom you can talk openly will make you a better manager and communicator, because you won't have to bottle up fears and frustrations and you'll be less likely to burden your team with those feelings.

People in your trust squad may function like therapists but can also serve as editors. Whether I was facing the White House press corps or an MSNBC audience, or even just managing large teams, my job has always demanded that I choose my words carefully and present them with confidence. But to get to that moment requires feeling just the opposite. Grasping new and complex issues requires me to feel vulnerable and ask a lot of questions, and I've found that searching for the right take is much easier in a collaborative workplace where you feel safe to explore. So find your Dana, your Katie, your Jen, or your Ben in whatever job you are in because it will make you better equipped to stand up to the critics, the frustrations, and yes, even the Kremlin.

11

Say More

How to listen actively and attentively, whether networking,
at dinner, or conducting an interview on television

Working off of one of my signature note cards to quickly brief President Obama before a 2012 event in Ohio.

As you may have already realized, the title of this book can be interpreted in a few ways. "Say more" doesn't mean more words. Quite the contrary. The phrase "say more," as in "can you say more on that?," is a great way to ask someone for clarification, information, or elaboration, and to show you are an active and present listener. The title is a call to communicate better. You can say more with less, which may sound counterintuitive. But hear me out.

When you're actively listening, you're not just receiving information; you're saying something even when you're not even speaking.

Listening skills will help you in pretty much every relationship—professional, personal, or some combination of the two. I promise you, better listening skills will make you a better partner. Just ask anyone who has been married a long time and gone through the process of discussing logistics with their spouse over and over again. (My advice is to review those plans, yet again, with as much patience and grace as possible.)

But being a good listener isn't just about having two ears and a decent attention span. It's about noticing cues that signal something might be up, responding to shifts in tone or topic appropriately, and knowing how to ask questions that open a space for discussion.

Being a better listener can also help you engage on a deeper level, whether in a private discussion or in a public forum. President Obama is famous for his big sweeping speeches. His speech at the 2004 Democratic convention is what made me want to work for him. But it isn't his speaking superpowers alone that enable him to connect with people.

Early on during his presidential campaign in 2007 he spent more time asking questions and hearing people explain their challenges than talking at them. He had started his career as a community organizer on the South Side of Chicago, where he honed his skills of engaging, listening, and building bridges that once seemed impossible. Being such an engaged listener is part of what he would say propelled a black man named Barack Hussein Obama to win over the voters in the mostly rural, mostly white state of Iowa. The voters there may have started out skeptical that a constitutional law professor who split his childhood between Indonesia and Hawaii had anything in common with them. But then he would sit at their kitchen table and ask them about their struggles with healthcare and at the right moment share that his own mother, who had died of cancer, had trouble getting access to good healthcare. He walked in parades in their small towns and knocked on doors and listened to parents talk about their hopes for their kids or their worries about their futures, and he could connect by sharing his own experience as a father of two young daughters. His ability and willingness to acknowledge that many people have little experience with those who are different from them was what made him such a great communicator across divides. He found a way to show people that he understood where they were coming from, helping them to set their skepticism aside and eventually listen to what he had to say.

The first step to being a better listener is simple: put down your phone, stop making your to-do list, and start paying attention. At a time when we all get caught up in our own schedules, and the many distractions of technology, noticing small details about another person, whether they're your boss, a colleague, your partner, your daughter's kindergarten teacher, or your daughter, means even more. Most people don't have poker faces. If you pay attention, you can tell when they need to say or hear more.

When I ask my kids how their day at school was, they typically say "fine" or "good" and just want to get back to whatever they were doing. I'd love more details, but the consistency tells me that I don't have anything to worry about or to push them on. But if they say, "It was great!" I always ask them to tell me more. And if they say, "I don't want to talk about it," I know I should pay attention and look for an opportunity to listen more.

This is true with friendships and certainly with colleagues. If you've been working with someone for a while, you can probably read their cues when they're frustrated, or tired, or displeased. (This is part of why I really struggled working from home during the pandemic—it was hard to pick up on tone and body language on Zoom.) Once you begin noticing these habits and behaviors, you'll also start noticing when things change. Sometimes the prompt can be an open-ended "What is worrying you the most right now?" or more declarative "I can see on your face that this isn't working for you." These are two easy ways to show you've been paying attention, and to create space for a deeper conversation about what might be troubling them. You'll be surprised at how these simple statements can help, particularly when someone *is* having a hard time or is reluctant to speak up when something, whether professional or personal, is bothering them.

Sometimes I take in other people's emotions too much—I get this from my mother, who is frequently sidelined by strangers at the supermarket wanting to share their life stories—and I pride myself on trying to sense when my friends, coworkers, and family have a problem they might want to be invited to talk about. It doesn't mean I'm always right—sometimes people are just tired, or their mind is on a conversation they had with their child or spouse, and whatever signal I thought they were giving is not a bigger sign of disconnect. But with certain people I've developed a good sense for when something's up. After years of working with President Obama, I knew when he was exasperated in a meeting because he had a tendency to lean back in his chair, put his arms behind his head, and puff out his cheeks. That was a clear sign he wanted the person who was talking to stop talking.

As press secretary I was always trying to keep an eye on the atmosphere of the press pool; a collective shuffling in seats meant I was going on too long. Although it's a little insulting to my ego, it wasn't unheard of for someone to fall asleep, and it doesn't take a communications expert to decipher the meaning of that. But they might have been up late on a deadline the night before (or just snoozing through a slow news day). I can admit that I also fell asleep during a few of my predecessors' briefings while sitting on the side of the room watching. I'm grateful that no photo evidence has yet been produced of me napping on the job.

I know I give a couple of cues that indicate disappointment, concern, displeasure, or worse. If I am not at all impressed with someone on a professional level, I almost always say something like "I know he means well," or "I know he is a nice person, but . . ." For some reason I feel the need to start with that caveat even though the people who know me well know that I am about to convey an opinion that is not at all flattering. There were times in the briefing room when I would get quiet and look directly at the person who was interrupting or derailing a briefing, usually with a slight tilt of my head. I would stand still—no encouraging nods or understanding looks. While people in the room may have thought I was just controlling my response, my friends and family knew that stare meant I was pissed off. The question "Are you done?" was usually implied.

Intellectually I knew that controlling my emotions was the only approach, most of the time. I was speaking on behalf of the government and wanted the day's stories to be about the message we were trying to deliver, not about me having an outburst. This wasn't always easy. As much as I liked and respected the vast majority of the reporters in the briefing room (including Peter Doocy), there could sometimes be a herd mentality in there, especially when the news was tough and the answers were limited. There were days when it seemed like the reporters were almost egging each other on, seeing who could be more combative, when I wanted to blurt out, "Are you fucking serious with this right now?" I envisioned those reporters high-fiving each other afterward, caring more about how they seemed to be standing up to power (which by the way involved asking me questions from a comfortable seat in the secure White House complex) than the subject at hand. But if I had cursed or called them out, it would have only made the situation worse, so my only option was to roll with it. I intently listened, and definitely glared.

Just as I might read into small changes in my friends' or colleagues' mannerisms, I've learned to use body language and facial expressions to emphasize a point, strengthen connections, or communicate something I might not be able to say out loud.

To prepare for the press secretary job, I studied not just what my predecessors said, but how they said it. For years while I was working at the White House I'd watched Robert Gibbs, Jay Carney, and Josh Earnest conduct briefings, and in the days leading up to Joe Biden's inauguration I reviewed footage of other press secretaries, too.

As I watched the recordings, I started noticing things I hadn't paid attention to when I was more focused on how to write my points for a briefing. Their control of their facial expressions often served as a sort of punctuation mark to what they were saying. It's obvious that you shouldn't be grinning ear to ear when you're talking about something like chemical weapons. You also don't want to look like you're annoyed or exasperated by whatever you're describing, or seem emotionless. You have to find an expression that acknowledges the horror while still being able to deliver the information. No matter the subject, nothing screams "phony" like a forced smile. And although the internet loves clips of someone losing their cool—by either yelling or even just being too short with a reporter—actually doing so promises to overshadow the content of what might have otherwise been a great press conference.

When you're trying to look like you're having a conversation even though you're speaking in front of a crowd, one of the tricks I've learned is that it helps to identify specific people in the audience and speak as if you're talking directly to them. You need to rotate among these people; otherwise, it looks like you're trying to send one random person in the audience a secret coded message and you may even freak them out: *Why is this ginger-haired lady staring at me so intensely?*

As the communications consultant Nick Morgan wrote in an article in the *Harvard Business Review*, "If your spoken message and your body language are mismatched, audiences will respond to the nonverbal message every time." It's a pretty bold claim, but it makes sense: the lie detector test is based on the idea that our bodies tell the truth when our words don't. Audiences have learned to interpret words and gestures together, and it's important to adapt your body language to your message. If you're telling a joke, or you have good news, it's fine to loosen up a bit; if what you have to say is serious, or somber, or even just disappointing, you have to be very careful about how you're holding yourself.

One of the biggest questions I have come across about body language is what to do with your hands, whether you're at a podium, posing for a picture, or sitting across from someone having a one-on-one. Media trainers, or people who teach others how to give public presentations and speeches and appear on television, will often say you should not move your hands at all, and I'm here to tell you: that's terrible advice. If you're like me, you can't help moving your hands—it's part of your personality. Certainly, too much hand movement can be distracting. But we all talk with our hands, and even the least naturally expressive person in the world will look like a malfunctioning robot if their hands are locked and immobile.

Body language can have a huge effect on how your message is received. Particularly if you're dealing with an audience who may not want to hear what you're saying, they'll be looking for reasons not to trust you and tense hands or weird posture will make them think you're not confident about your message. When sitting at a table, many people opt for resting one hand over the other, or holding a pen and a notebook. Clasping your hands is one of those things that seem like an easy choice, comfortable and sending a signal that you're smart and sophisticated, but it's really hard to do without looking like you are under duress.

Making your body language feel natural and not robotic is essential for both you and your audience; it's another reason why practicing your delivery in a physical space that resembles the real thing is so useful—you'll only know how uncomfortable it feels to sit through a fifteen-minute job interview with your hands clasped under the table the whole time once you've tried it out. Just to save you the trouble, I can tell you it is not natural or comfortable.

If people start paying more attention to how you're walking or sitting or tilting your head or clasping your hands, they're not going to pay as close attention to what you're saying. They're going to be distracted when they should be invested in the conversation. And if *you* start thinking too much about how you're walking or sitting, et cetera, you're not going to be fully focused on what you're saying. You're going to be listening to yourself, not your audience.

When I started at MSNBC, one observation during early practice sessions was that I leaned in a lot—I was moving forward, toward the interview subjects, often so far I was going out of the camera shot. I was advised I should try to dial it back. But over time it became clear that leaning in was part of how I listened and engaged. Losing the lean would suppress my ability to connect. While some interviewers do a grave, slow nod to respond to a subject's difficult story, there are other ways to be present for the subject without interrupting them with verbal encouragement. My leaning shows that I'm paying attention to the person I'm talking to, and that I'm fully engaged in our conversation. It is sending the message that they are saying something so interesting I am getting closer to hear more. So if you are watching my show and I am suddenly leaning so far in that I am out of the camera shot, it probably means the person I am interviewing is saying something really interesting and you might want to turn up the volume.

Sending a message that you're actively listening is also a way of showing empathy. Although I've been interviewed many times, I hadn't thought so much about what it was like on the other side until I left the White House. It's a completely different experience! When you're being interviewed, you can often follow the interviewer's lead—it's primarily a balance of responding to the questions and delivering your intended message, to the best of your ability, based on what they ask. This requires serious listening skills. All the prep work I did before starting as White House press secretary certainly made me better at things like dealing with confrontational reporters, but it also reminded me why conventional strategies don't always work; they're usually more about finding a shortcut and controlling the conversation than about actual effective communication.

One common tip I think is particularly hazardous is the famous PR dictum to "answer the question you want to answer, not the question you were asked." That sounds clever, and if you can pull it off, good for you. But the problem is that if you're answering what you wished you'd been asked, you're often missing the mark with your audience and you come across like you didn't actually listen to the question. "You have to put yourself in the other person's shoes," the presentation coach Burt Alper says. "If someone took a reframe too far and started answering a different question, how would that make you feel? You would feel either unappreciated or unheard, or it might even make you think less of the person who is trying to communicate in the first place because they didn't seem like they were able to manage your question." Avoiding an interviewer's questions will make them and the audience feel disrespected, or even insulted—do you think they aren't smart enough to notice your not-so-subtle evasions?

Understanding what it's like to be interviewed allowed me to put myself in the subject's shoes when I started working as an anchor. But there was still a learning curve. Interviewing someone means having responsibility for the overall tone and trajectory of the conversation, and you have to maintain both flexibility and a sense of control for when things may be veering off track. Since true engagement isn't a one-way street, your success at conducting an interview you've meticulously researched, scripted, and practiced often depends on how well you can adapt when things don't go according to plan, like when your subject raises a totally unexpected issue, makes a great point out of left field, or starts to get emotional. This is when listening skills are most important— they prepare you to go along with a conversation as it's happening. Being able to listen when you have a range of things on your mind, including what other questions to ask and how much time you have left, is one of the most important skills an interviewer can have. It is far easier to just meticulously follow a list of planned questions, but that leaves no room for truly engaging with the person sitting across from you.

As you know by now, I'm a prepper. I sometimes try to pretend I'm not. I work hard at conveying an easy, breezy, go with the flow vibe at work, but I am definitely on the type A end of the spectrum. My close friends and family would tell you that in my personal life I can veer in the opposite direction, closer to absentminded professor in a constant search for my wallet, car keys, train ticket, and sometimes even my actual car in a parking lot. But work is a different story.

When you're as obsessed with being prepared, and I know a lot of people are, it can be difficult to let go and be totally present in a conversation. You have a list of ten points you want to cover and only seven or eight minutes to get to them. But the plan has to serve the conversation, not the other way around. If the person you're speaking to says something very interesting in response to your fourth question, you have to be willing to throw out the rest of your notes and see where the conversation leads. You have to leave space to listen. If you're thinking of an interview as a box-checking exercise, you're not having a conversation. One of my bosses at MSNBC, Greg Kordick, gave me a great piece of advice (one of many he has given me) when I first started that I've repeated to others: Nobody at home knows your plan. This means that you don't have to worry about going off script; no one will ever know, or be disappointed. It will be more disappointing if you don't go where an interesting conversation is taking itself.

Whether you're conducting an interview or simply taking the initiative to broach a difficult conversation, it's crucial that you pay attention and respond to what your conversation partner is actually saying. When you do that, the conversation might lead you to surprising places. There's no shame in asking for clarification if you don't understand something someone said, or repeating what they've said to confirm you've gotten it right, or even pausing to repeat an interesting or a surprising point they are making—it indicates that you care about their message and you're not just going through the motions. This flexibility gives you the space to respond authentically, as a fellow human being. As an interviewer, I've definitely had moments when I had a hard time holding back tears because of the subject matter or the emotional force of my subject's words. Speaking to people who have just lost loved ones to war or political violence, for example, will always be difficult, but it's my duty as an interviewer to be fully present in those conversations.

The best interviews don't turn a corner to reveal a gotcha. A successful public conversation is about moving beyond the caricatures most public figures find themselves confined by and giving them space to surprise you, and your audience.

Sometimes you plan for a fight that never comes. I recently interviewed Chris Christie, and I was so ready for an argument—but that's not what we did. I was prepared to have to fact-check him on every other line, but when he didn't say anything incorrect, it meant our conversation could go to new places: instead of wasting time debating a point that most viewers at home would know their opinion about in advance, I was able to ask tough questions about everything from Trump's lead in the polls to abortion. Twitter might love a clip of people fighting, but people at home can tell if it is a performance and not actually a productive form of communication.

People in your life can surprise you in this way, too; sometimes you might be ready to fight tooth and nail not to go out to dinner again with a particular couple, and when you finally bring up the subject to your partner after dreading the conversation, they just smile and respond, "I'm *so* glad you said that. I don't want to go to dinner with them either!"

I'm not advocating that you wing it when you have to conduct an interview or have an important conversation, or that your partner will always agree with you on how to spend your Saturday nights. But instead of getting fixated on a specific plan that makes you unmovable, it helps to think about your goals for the conversation: Do you want your best friend to tell you more about why she skipped your birthday party last week? Do you want an apology, and nothing less will suffice? Do you want to debate a politician about their vote on an issue, or to learn more about what drives them to hold that position?

You might come up with any number of goals for a conversation, but you should also come up with a list of priorities: maybe some topics are essential, while others would be nice to cover. Regardless, effective communication is about adapting, and the best conversations can't be totally planned out in advance.

* * *

Whether you're watching George Stephanopoulos follow up on policy details in a tough interview or listening to Glennon Doyle dig deeper on an emotional point on her podcast, the more you observe great communicators in action, the more you notice how well they listen. Yes, it's strange to say that you can watch or hear someone listening, but with some people, you actually can. Paying attention is a full-body exercise, and a lot of it comes back to being present in the moment. The best listeners do much more than nod. They probe; they engage; they seek more information. And they make the experience of listening collaborative and interactive. You can prepare, read, plan, and write for hours in advance, but that's all in service of this one goal. What all great communicators have in common is their ability to make people feel heard. You can read all the parenting books, attend every parent-teacher conference, and cull advice from friends all you want—what kids want is for you to be present, paying attention, and trying to understand what they're saying to you.

The same is true of politicians. A truly gifted politician will make whoever they're speaking to feel like they're the only person in the room. And most of the time it is because the politician is doing less of the talking and more of the listening.

The President Biden who is privately negotiating a contentious issue with world leaders and the President Biden who is speaking to fellow parishioners after Sunday church services are obviously the same person, but while a transcript of the negotiations would give you a good sense of the Joe Biden who speaks with world leaders, a written summary of his exchanges with a community hit by a natural disaster, or a family that has lost a loved one, would fail to show a sensitivity that can't be captured on paper. His ability to be present reflects his authentic capacity for empathy, which shows through in his gestures, pauses, and demeanor.

For politicians, the ability to listen at public events and respond accordingly is also a powerful form of communicating. One of the most memorable moments from the late senator John McCain's presidential campaign in 2008 was not a speech he gave at the convention or a lengthy attack he had prepared against Obama; it was a moment in a town hall meeting when a woman in the audience started making claims about Barack Obama's character and even his nationality. It was weeks before election day. McCain was trailing in the polls. It would have been easy for him to let her continue speaking and even to cheer her on. But instead, McCain grabbed the microphone and said, "No ma'am, he's a decent family man, citizen, that I just happen to have disagreements with on fundamental issues." McCain responded not as a politician but as a human being. Some people in the audience booed him, but that brief moment said more about McCain's character and also his legacy than most other public speeches he delivered.

My most memorable day of all my years working at the White House was not my first briefing (though that was pretty exhilarating) on Inauguration Day. It was a day late in June of 2016, I was eight and a half months pregnant, and the Supreme Court had ruled in favor of marriage equality. I remember standing to the side of the Rose Garden watching President Obama speak and thinking the day could not get better. But what was most memorable was not actually anything he said about marriage equality. It was something he did a few hours later.

He had been scheduled to travel to Charleston for the funeral of Reverend Clementa Pinckney and eight other parishioners who died in the anti-black mass shooting at Mother Emanuel Church. He wanted to attend the funeral but did not want to give a speech initially because he didn't know what more he could say to address gun violence or to heal the pain of this community. He ended up delivering the eulogy at the service, but it wasn't his words that connected with the congregation that day; it was the moment he started singing. He understood in that moment that even a shaky voice singing "Amazing Grace" was what the people in the church, who also had no words to express their grief, needed to hear.

I watched from a small television outside my office and felt the tears streaming down my face. More than anything I felt pride. Proud to be standing there. Proud to have come back to the White House. And proud to work for the person leading that congregation in song.

When I walked out of the White House gates that night, I could see the final touches of our celebration of the marriage equality ruling being put together. The entire White House was lit up in rainbow colors, and hundreds of people gathered outside to celebrate the recognition of their love. That image was more powerful than any words.

Effective communication is about cracking the door open to learn more, and to expand the perspective of an audience you are trying to reach. It is about evoking emotion. And in order to do that you need to be much more than an effective talker. You need to be an effective listener.

I first learned about "active listening" way back when I was knocking on doors in Iowa, though it probably wasn't called that at the time. In our training, we were coached to be fully present, to ask questions that encouraged responses, and, more than anything, to seek understanding. We weren't there to argue a point, even if some of the people who opened their doors assumed that's what we were trying to do. Most people know how important it is to be present for a conversation, but actually doing that for hours a day, several days a week, showed me how truly *active* active listening can be. It also showed me that these methods work. Once you learn to listen and be in the moment, the people you're communicating with will begin to say more.

Taking Questions

On answering tough questions effectively and honestly

Some of my most important communication happens at home (or on family vacations, like this one in Colorado).

One night, during the early weeks of the Russian invasion of Ukraine, my daughter wanted to ask me a few questions. It was already past her bedtime, but part of our nightly routine was her asking me three questions. These questions ranged from "Who has the longest hair in the world?" to "How many kinds of fish are there in the ocean?" Sometimes I could answer off the top of my head, and sometimes we needed to consult my phone. On this particular night the tone was more serious. We were lying side by side on the trundle bed in my son's bedroom, where she slept every night despite having her own room simply because she liked being closer to her brother. The room was dark, the night-light reflecting stars on the ceiling.

"Why do wars start?"

The mix of emotions I felt in that moment was profound. I was sad that my six-year-old daughter had somehow heard about the war, and I was daunted at the prospect of answering a question that experts in international relations have been debating for decades. I wanted to be honest with her, but I didn't know how I'd translate the message into language she could understand. I was also exhausted. I'd been in meetings about what was happening on the ground in the region all day, and I'd been briefing the White House press corps about what the United States and other countries were doing to support Ukraine for weeks. I'd hoped tucking my child in would be a break from war talk, but apparently I was still taking questions on the subject.

"Wars start for different reasons," I said. "Sometimes it's about a difference of views on a personal issue, like religion. And sometimes it's about one side wanting the other side's land."

Not bad, I thought. But she had a follow-up. "How are wars won?" she asked.

"Well," I said, "sometimes wars are fought for years and aren't resolved. Sometimes a lot of people are hurt in the process. And sometimes there's a negotiation, or basically a conversation, and they agree to terms that will end it."

She seemed to take this in. Then she said she had one more question. I braced myself.

"Have you ever seen a real unicorn?" she asked.

Once in a while, you get thrown a softball.

"I wish," I responded.

* * *

It's easy to look at someone standing at a podium with a big briefing book, or an executive sitting in a fancy chair at the head of the fancy conference room table, or a star professor in front of a crowded lecture hall and think that what they're doing has nothing to do with the conversations that go on in the back of the room, around the office coffee machine, or at your child's bedside at 8:00 p.m. But the same rules for successful communication apply to everyone. Engagement is a process, and the words you say might not always be as important as the way you make people feel. When I think about the great communicators I've met, some aren't people who ever ran for office, or were even comfortable in the spotlight. But they were optimists: they believe that connection is possible, and they strive for it because they think something good will come of it.

I wasn't sure I'd handled my daughter's questions about war as well as I could have until a few days later, when I heard her talking to her little brother.

"Hey, buddy," she said. "Did you know wars sometimes start because people want their neighbors' land? That's crazy, isn't it?" Great communication skills are more like building blocks than steps on a checklist. You can't craft a message if you don't know your audience; you can't know your audience if you don't research; you can't deliver the message if you haven't developed trust and credibility as a speaker; you can't build credibility if you don't accept feedback graciously, correct yourself when you make a mistake, or set realistic boundaries. It all takes an enormous amount of work. Every single great communicator I know doesn't just show up and speak—they work at it. They adapt when they make mistakes. They spend time becoming a version of an expert on the subjects they are talking about, on their delivery, and on the way they connect with their intended audience. That applies whether you are planning to conduct briefings from a podium, speaking in front of a boardroom, or just trying to find more effective ways to talk to your partner.

Was the conversation my daughter and I had about the war more important than President Biden's conversation with Volodymyr Zelensky? To the world, absolutely not, by a factor of infinity. In retrospect, it may not have even been that important to my daughter. But my bedtime briefing—short, crisp, jargon-free, and audience appropriate—had been a success. My daughter felt listened to, and my message had been heard.

So I'm ready for my next challenge: a briefing on why eating vegetables is good for you. I know my audience. I've done my prep work. I've thought about what questions they might ask, what objections they might have, and what I can do to establish my credibility on the issue. And if all else fails, I'll remind them that "unicorns love spinach. No, I've never met one, but Joe Biden told me. Remember, he's that man who bakes great cookies?"

Acknowledgments

One of the most important lessons of effective communications is expressing gratitude, and I have a great deal of it.

I will be forever grateful to Nan Graham for the opportunity to write this book. Nan is an institution, and the first time I spoke with her, I was nervous. If you've read the book you know that I wrote out what I wanted to say in advance. But I learned through the course of writing that she is not only tough and brilliant, but also warm and insightful.

Kara Watson took on the editing of a book written by someone who had never written a book before. I feel comfortable confirming on her behalf that that is not an easy task. She never lost her cool through the ups and downs, and I am grateful she was on this journey.

I would not have even written this book had it not been for a conversation with Pilar Queen, who convinced me that a book about what I wish I'd known twenty years ago, one that would empower others to become stronger communicators, was actually a greater contribution than a tell-all (if you've read the book and didn't just skip to the acknowledgments, you know that is not my style).

Pilar and Georgia Bodnar both reassured me throughout the publishing process, and I am grateful to both of them for sticking with me even on the days where I was doubtful of their confidence.

I am grateful to have had a few incredible guides along the way. Nell Scovell helped me figure out how to tell stories at the beginning of the process. Geoff Shandler helped me better understand how to integrate bigger-picture ideas.

Then there is Lauren Oyler, who is like Mariano Rivera (for the non–baseball followers out there he is a famous closing pitcher) and Mariah Carey's voice coach wrapped into one. Lauren helped me tap into the thousands of stories I have and helped them make sense in a book. I would never want to be on the other end of one of her famous literary critiques. But I am grateful that she was my partner in finalizing the book.

Many thanks to the rest of the team at Scribner, particularly Emily Polson, Stu Smith, Brian Belfiglio, Paul Samuelson, Brianna Yamashita, Mark LaFlaur, and Jaya Miceli.

To my colleagues at MSNBC, especially Rebecca Kutler and Greg Kordick, for making me better at what I do every time I talk with them. To Rashida Jones for never asking me to be anyone other than who I am, and for believing I could indeed learn how to use a teleprompter— thank you. And a special shout-out to Alex Lupica, Margaret Menefee, and Will Rabbe, and the entire *Inside with Jen Psaki* team. There is not a smarter, harder-working and more thoughtful group, and we would not have a show without them. I am grateful that they took the leap with me.

A number of people in my professional life have been beacons of light and sometimes of tough talk—people who pushed me, encouraged me, and rooted for me over the course of my career. I couldn't name them all and certainly will forget some here. But my political gurus have taught me that sticking your neck out for people who work for you and looking out for them even when it is inconvenient is the sign of a great boss. To Jeff Zients, David Axelrod, Ron Klain, Denis McDonough, Rahm Emanuel, Linda Douglass, David Plouffe, Anita

Dunn, Robert Gibbs, Dan Pfeiffer, Bill Burton, and David Wade, thank you for being great bosses and gurus. I learned many things from all of you.

And to people who took chances on me: President Joe Biden, thank you for believing I could tap into your voice, and Dr. Jill Biden, thanks for trusting me to stand up for what you have been working so hard for over the years.

Thank you to the incredible Biden press team I had the honor of working with during one of the most challenging first years of a presidency: Amanda Finney, Karine Jean-Pierre, Andrew Bates, Chris Meagher, TJ Ducklo, Mike Gwin, Emilie Simons, Brittany Caplin, Vedant Patel, Kevin Munoz, Michael Kikukawa, Angela Dela Cruz, Natalie Austin, and Megha Bhattacharya.

Obama staff, forever family. You are so big and expansive! We are a lifelong extended family, and I appreciate all of you.

Secretary John Kerry, I will be forever grateful for your optimism and your belief that there is always a pony at the bottom of the pile of manure.

And to President Barack Obama, who to this day reminds us that politics is about hope, and about one person in one room making a difference. The ten years I spent working for you continue to guide who I am today.

To my own personal trust squad, my friends who could care less whether I am briefing from a podium or not, but root for me regardless: Ally Wagner, Denise Abella, Meg Pomfret, Erica Caldwell, Maggie Ball, Mandy Trucksess, Trish Ripley, Jenni and Theo LeCompte, Jess and Ragan Naresh, Katie McCormick Lelyveld and Tim Malatesta, Tom and Aretae Wyler, Kate Bedingfield, Adrienne Elrod, Dana Remus and Brett Holmgren, and many more I will definitely regret not including, but promise to make it up to them.

And last, but most important, my family.

To my dad for instilling a sense of fearlessness and endless curiosity in all of us. A vacation with you is still exhausting.

To my sisters, Stephanie and Kristen. Though you are both younger than me, you are often wiser, and you force me to think differently and more expansively about the world.

To my mom for always being the voice making me a better person, who taught me that even when you have your wings, your roots are what keep you grounded.

To my husband, Greg. I can't imagine doing this life without you. I still pinch myself that I get to be on this roller coaster with you.

And to my kids, Vivi and Matthew. The saying goes that your heart lives outside of your body when you have children. My heart will always live outside of mine. This book is really for you.

Notes

18 *"What story could I tell"*: Kelly McGonigal, in "Feeling Nervous? How Anxiety Can Fuel Better Communication," *Think Fast, Talk Smart* podcast, October 11, 2022, https://www.gsb.stanford.edu /insights/feeling-nervous-how-anxiety-can-fuel-better-commu nication.

96 *"you'll be thought of as intelligent"*: Daniel M. Oppenheimer, "Consequences of Erudite Vernacular Utilized Irrespective of Necessity: Problems with Using Long Words Needlessly," *Applied Cognitive Psychology* 20, no. 2 (March 2006): 153.

99 *"what a patient might call their 'bedside manner'"*: Jill Suttie, "Should We Train Doctors for Empathy?," *Greater Good Magazine*, Greater Good Science Center/University of California, Berkeley, July 8, 2015.

99 *doctors and nurses never effectively explained:* E. Brooke Lerner, Dietrich V. K. Jehle, David M. Janicke, and Ronald M. Moscati, "Medical Communication: Do Our Patients Understand?," *American Journal of Emergency Medicine* 18, no. 7 (November 2000).

102 *"'we're so sorry, we messed up'"*: Daniel Pink, in "No Regrets: How to Take Risks in Your Communication, Relationships, and Career,"

Think Fast, Talk Smart podcast, May 30, 2023, https://www.gsb .stanford.edu/insights/no-regrets-how-take-risks-your-communi cation-relationships-career.

124 *"virtually every domain in which humans deal with humans":* Geoffrey L. Cohen, *Belonging: The Science of Creating Connection and Bridging Divides* (New York: W. W. Norton, 2022), x.

124 *they didn't like Obamacare but did like the ACA:* "Six of One— Obamacare vs. the Affordable Care Act," *Jimmy Kimmel Live,* https://www.youtube.com/watch?v=sx2scvIFGjE&t=4s.

Photo Credits

1 Official White House Photo by Chandler West

11 Official White House Photo by Cameron Smith

29 Official White House Photo by Cameron Smith

49 Official White House Photo by Pete Souza

73 Official White House Photo by Adam Schultz

95 Courtesy of the author

115 Courtesy of the author

131 Official White House Photo by Cameron Smith

147 Courtesy of the author

163 Courtesy of Jason and Yeganeh Rezaian

179 Official White House Photo by Adam Schultz

199 Official White House Photo by Pete Souza

215 Courtesy of the author